Bc

DC 91 .S413
Sepet, Marius.
Saint Louis

The Saints

SAINT LOUIS

Authorised Translation
All Rights Reserved

SAINT LOUIS

BY

MARIUS SEPET

WITH A PREFACE BY
GEORGE TYRRELL, S.J.

LONDON
DUCKWORTH & CO., 3, HENRIETTA STREET, W.C.

NEW YORK, CINCINNATI & CHICAGO:
BENZIGER BROS.

DUBLIN:
M. H. GILL & SO

1899

DC
91
.S413

AUTHOR'S PREFACE

THE plan adopted in this volume demands a word of explanation. The reader must not look for a history of St Louis, that is, for a chronological and methodical account of the actions of his life and the events of his reign. This would not, in our opinion, correspond to the general design of the collection in which this essay is to find a place. We have thought it better to make a study of the character and sanctity of this great Christian and royal person, considered under the different aspects of his private and public life. It has been our ideal to present to our readers a series of historic pictures in stained glass, devoted to the life of St Louis.

In the different compartments of this series, or, to speak without metaphor, in the successive chapters of this work, we have made large use of the text of writers contemporary with the holy king, necessarily made intelligible to modern readers. We have also given as far as possible the very words of the holy king. Nothing throws more light on the mind of St Louis than his *Instructions* to his son Philip and to his daughter Isabel. We cannot know and describe him better than his confessor, Geoffrey of Beaulieu, his chaplain, William of Chartres, and the confessor of his wife, Queen Margaret, whose writings afford such a valuable summary of the inquiry made for his canonisation. Wherever it was possible we have used the words of the Sire de Joinville, the good seneschal, who has in our own day found an editor and interpreter worthy of him in the person of M. Natalis de Wailly. We hope that our quotations may induce our readers to draw more largely and directly from this incomparable source which now flows with limpid clearness.

From a somewhat different point of view we feel the same desire with respect to the valuable works which have guided us in the choice and reproduction of the original texts, and which have supplemented these texts. Since the reader will not find here a history of St Louis, it may be sought in the interesting books which are quoted in the ensuing pages. We feel that we shall not have laboured in vain if we add to the readers of M. Wailly, of M. Felix Faure and M. Lecoy de la Marche. We must also mention particularly M. Elie Berger's remarkable work on Blanche of Castile, and on the relations between Louis IX. and Innocent IV. A Protestant by birth and education, we wish that others of the same religion understood as well as he does the duty of historic impartiality, and the respect due from all good Frenchmen to the national religion and the catholic glories of their country. We have also profited, although not without reserve, from the sincere homage recently rendered by an honest freethinker, M. Ch. Langlois, to St Louis's memory in a Parisian review.

An appearance of learned research is not altogether

AUTHOR'S PREFACE

suitable to the collection of which this volume forms a part. But in a study conducted on these lines the case is rather exceptional. The reference to so many authors cannot be troublesome to the reader, and we flatter ourselves that this little book, in addition to its special and immediate object, may be useful to future historians of St Louis as a storehouse of information. So noble a subject cannot indeed fail to become increasingly attractive to men of capable minds and descriptive powers. We wish the glory of St Louis, like that of Joan of Arc, to increase ever more and more in France.

EDITOR'S PREFACE

"IT may be asserted," says a modern writer, "that since the days of St Louis one movement has, in the main, continued almost uninterruptedly, in spite of actions of an apparently conflicting tendency. This process has been one of continuous disintegration of the medieval Christian theocracy, proceeding with varying degrees of rapidity over the whole area of what was once Christendom."

It is as standing almost on the very line dividing the old order from the new, and, as being himself so choice a sample of the best produce of medieval Christianity, that St Louis claims special attention. The pagan naturalism that is inborn in the Aryan peoples, if not to some extent in all decadent humanity, had been crushed and overlaid by a superimposed religion of Semitic type, with which it could no more blend than water with oil; but it was there none the less, seeking issue and release at every crevice or crack that offered itself. The Church had set her heel on the serpent's head, but life was still vigorous though ineffectual. In that hour she seemed all but victorious; yet it was just then, in the moment of her security, that her foe was to begin slipping from her power to renew the battle again and again on fresh ground, and by fresh methods. For it is not by steady advance, but by shock and countershock between false and true, by alternating defeat and victory, that an idea like Christianity forces its way to perfect expression.

Time after time the work so nearly finished, so seemingly fair, is rudely unravelled by the Master, to be wrought again from the beginning, for the sake of some blemish, some inwoven strand of alien texture, that mars its unity and consistency. Medieval theocratic society had not separated so distinctly and consciously its own governing principle from that of the paganism it had superseded, as to detect at once the intrusion, into its own system, of germs destructive of its health and life.

In St Louis we have the medieval ideal of a monarch realised as nearly as possible. Not, of course, but that he had faults and limitations of character as every saint has; or that he did not, in virtue of his surroundings, reflect the ruggedness and even the fierceness of his age. "Then the pious king ordered the said woman to be burned at Pontoise, in despite of all prayers, and so she was" (p. 193). This makes us shudder, just as our calm indifference to far worse forms of cruelty would have thrilled the soul of Louis with indignation. Still, if we take sanctity in the widest sense, as meaning heroic, superhuman, sustained conscientiousness, perhaps there is no one of any creed or credence who will dispute the saintship of Louis; especially when we remember what the opportunities and temptations of an absolute monarch in the Middle Ages must have been, and how few, as a fact, were able to withstand them. But sanctity has many moulds and shapes, being but another name for supernatural perfection, and perfection being a term relative to the thing to be perfected. It is not merely as a man, but as a king, that Louis reached the standard of heroic perfection as conceived in his day.

The essential idea of theocracy is the supremacy of conscience, of right, of duty, over the State; that there is a judge over every earthly judge, to whose tribunal every man, the least and feeblest, as well as the greatest, has right of appeal against force, and oppression, and tyranny; that no man, as man, has coercive right over his fellows, but solely as the delegate of God or of conscience.

Aquinas, in whose teaching the Catholic idea then found its clearest and most advanced expression, while he held, what perhaps none would deny, that monarchy was the fittest form of government, given a man fit to wield it—given a Christ—was also clear in affirming that, to every reasonably appointed government, God lent his divine power and authority, in obedience to the exigencies of man's social nature. In this sense, the right of a democracy was as divine as that of the crowned and anointed emperor; both were from God, but dependent on God, and powerless, not only against Christ or his Church, but against the clear conscience of the meanest peasant. The same apostles who bade men see and obey God in the secular and pagan rulers entrusted by him with the sword of justice, set limit to this obedience when it came in conflict with conscience: "Judge ye whether it be just in the sight of God that we should obey you rather than God." This is a conception excluded by a godless naturalism, whose issue is necessarily the despotism of the many over the few; of the strong, the rich, the fortunate, over the wretched, the poor, and the weak. Loyal and true as he was in holding his sceptre subject to the superior claims of conscience, of Christ, and of the international Church of Christendom, whereof France was but a member, yet, partly owing to a current and easy misinterpretation of an ecclesiastical ceremony, "St Louis's fervour inclined him to consider that the unction of his consecration invested the kingship with spiritual and almost sacerdotal privileges." As M. Sepet points out, "the distinction between the spiritual and temporal orders was, at that time, much less clearly understood and defined than has since been the case, in the teaching of theology, philosophy, and politics"; and it was this very confusion which gave an opening for pagan despotism to creep out once more, and to substitute itself gradually in place of Christian monarchy, until, at the great Revolution, the stifled and blinded sense of man's inalienable rights broke out in wild and half-suicidal frenzy, and shattered the imposture to pieces.

We have only to look to Russia to see how the investiture of supreme government in one man, and the consecration of that man by seemingly sacramental rites—which could not possibly be conferred on a democracy or an aristocracy—favours the idea that his right is divine in a sense denied to those forms of government—in a priestly and supernatural sense. We can see there, how, what is professedly a Christian theocracy can degenerate into a practical despotism, pagan in principle, through the enslavement of the Church to the State, and the sacrifice of that liberty which she can secure only by being cosmopolitan. We can then understand how, in the very highest medieval ideal of monarchy, as conceived and realised by St Louis, there lurked a confusion — a scarce perceptible mustard-seed of error—a little cloud no larger than a man's hand, yet pregnant with the coming tempest.

And if it saddens us to think that a canker-worm can lie in the heart of the sweetest rose; that even saints may unconsciously and blamelessly sow tares along with their wheat, there is hope and counter-comfort in the thought, that the worst of God's enemies love him somewhat, and serve Him in spite of themselves, and, that while evil in the long-run neutralises evil, good re-enforces good.

G. TYRRELL.

CONTENTS

I. THE MAN

CHAPTER I

	PAGE
THE SON—ST LOUIS AND BLANCHE OF CASTILE—CHARACTER AND EDUCATION OF ST LOUIS .	1

CHAPTER II

THE HUSBAND—MARGARET OF PROVENCE . 15

CHAPTER III

THE FATHER AND BROTHER—THE ROYAL PRINCES AND PRINCESSES 27

CHAPTER IV

THE FRIEND AND MASTER—JOHN, SIRE DE JOINVILLE—ST LOUIS'S FOLLOWERS . . 41

CHAPTER V

THE CHRISTIAN—RELIGIOUS AND MORAL VIRTUES OF ST LOUIS 71

CHAPTER VI

THE CLERK — INTELLECTUAL QUALITIES AND HABITS OF ST LOUIS 89

CHAPTER VII

THE ASCETIC AND THE APOSTLE—TRANSCENDENT VIRTUES OF ST LOUIS 98

II. THE KING

CHAPTER I

THE KNIGHT AND THE COMMANDER—THE EARLY WARS OF ST LOUIS 126

CHAPTER II

THE TWO CRUSADES 131

CHAPTER III

THE GOVERNMENT OF ST LOUIS—INTERNAL POLICY 158

CHAPTER IV

FOREIGN POLICY 198

CHAPTER V

COMPARISON OF THE PUBLIC AND PRIVATE VIRTUES OF ST LOUIS—GENERAL CHARACTERISTICS AND RESULTS OF HIS REIGN . 209

CHAPTER VI

ST LOUIS IN HIS OWN DAY, AND IN THE EYES OF POSTERITY 218

SAINT LOUIS

I. THE MAN

CHAPTER I

THE SON—ST LOUIS AND BLANCHE OF CASTILE
CHARACTER AND EDUCATION OF ST LOUIS

LOUIS of France, whom France and the Christian world has venerated for six centuries under the name of St Louis, was born at Poissy on April 25th, 1214, the year of the victory of Bouvines. His grandfather, the great Philip Augustus, then occupied the throne. His father, Louis, the hereditary prince, had married, on May 23rd, 1200, a Spanish princess, Blanche, the daughter of Alphonso VIII., king of Castile, who brought him a numerous family. Their eldest son Philip, born in 1209, died when only eight or nine years old, and when Louis VIII. ascended the throne in 1223, the young Louis became heir-presumptive.

This heritage fell to him all too soon. Louis VIII. died at Montpensier on November 8th, 1226, when returning from the expedition into Languedoc which he had undertaken to stamp out the Albigense heresy. His short reign does not allow us to judge him as a king. As a man and as a Christian he seems to have gained the esteem and respectful admiration of his contemporaries by the exercise of solid and tactful virtues. He was specially renowned for his courage, piety, and conjugal fidelity. But he cannot have exerted any strong influence over his son, who was only twelve years old when called to succeed him.

This was not the case with Blanche of Castile. Born with the genius of a great statesman, this princess was also a model among mothers. Her regency had, politically, all the qualities and results of a reign. As a pupil of her father-in-law, Philip Augustus, she maintained and consolidated his work, shaken by the premature death of Louis VIII. and by the difficulties of a minority. By her firm views, her rapid decision and energetic action, she thwarted the repeated conspiracies of the feudal aristocracy; she sustained and still more firmly established the Capetian dynasty in the high position acquired to the great advantage of the nation, during the preceding reigns. "Blanche," says Berger, her most recent historian, "did wonders in bringing the great nobles to respect her son's authority and in defending general interests against private ambition. When Louis IX. reached his majority no one in France was—at least for the moment—in a position to rise up against him. The integrity of the royal dominions, for an instant in danger, had been maintained; Blois, Chartres, Sancerre and Châteaudun, the ancient fiefs of the dukes of Champagne, now belonged to the king alone; two new provinces had been added by the Treaty of

Paris to those which Louis had inherited from his father. All the possessions still remaining to the Court of Toulouse were, on his death, to revert to the House of France, which was now predominant on the left bank of the Rhone; and the great feudatories hitherto so threatening, had henceforth only to behave like respectful vassals."

When Blanche had, by degrees and almost insensibly, handed over the government to her son whom she had trained to its exercise, she remained in the natural order of things, without usurpation or affectation, his chief adviser and almost his associate on the throne. It is no exaggeration to say that Louis did nothing without her. Against her will he started for the Crusades, but he entrusted to her the regency of the kingdom with very extensive powers. She continued to exercise these powers until her death, never shrinking from the burden, much as she felt its weight. "Until the end of her life," says her historian, "she remained, as she had ever been, an active and energetic woman, a strict and just queen, doing all things herself and neglecting nothing when it was a question of maintaining the rights and dignity of the Crown."

Her death was that of a true Christian. "She was at Melun when, in November 1252, the heart-disease from which she suffered suddenly assumed so grave a character that she had herself transported hastily to Paris. There she took to her bed for the last time. In preparation for death she had put all her affairs in order, and had given instructions to compensate, out of her own personal fortune, all whom she might have wronged. Then she forgot her life of weariness and sorrow to think only of the rest of another life.

"Five or six days before her end, she received Communion from the bishop of Paris, Renaud de Corbeil, and the same day he gave her the Cistercian habit worn by the nuns of Maubuisson. The bishop, when giving her this humble clothing, told her that in the event of her death she should retain it; to which she replied that it was her desire to be a Religious in life and in death; and indeed, from that moment she became, until her last breath, as the humblest sister under the rule of the Abbess of Maubuisson. When she had received the last Sacraments she was carried by her attendants to a straw bed, covered with a simple serge cloth, for she seemed to have lost the power of speech and to be at the last extremity. The priests and clerks around her remained silent, thinking she was dead, but suddenly she began to repeat, in a low and feeble voice, the Prayers for the dying: 'Subvenite sancti Dei.' 'Hasten to help me, Saints of God.' Those present continued to say the prayers, but she had barely 'muttered between closed teeth' five or six verses when her soul departed.

"It was on the 26th or 27th November, probably towards three in the afternoon, that Blanche of Castile found in death the peace of which her life was almost always deprived. She had lived a little less than sixty-five years. She was lamented by the nation, and mainly by the lower classes. 'The common people sorrowed for her death,' say the

Chronicles of St Denis with simple eloquence, 'for she would have had them all rich, and she was strictly just.'"

History teaches us that women exceptionally gifted with a masculine character are apt to sacrifice to it their duties and family affections. But it was not so with Queen Blanche, who, on the contrary, fulfilled her duties as wife and mother all the better because she was able to regard them in fitting connection with her rank and royal duty. She herself superintended, with the needful counsel and assistance, the education of her children, and more particularly of the young king for whom she held herself to be responsible, in a very special manner, towards God, the nation, and the Royal House. She brought St Louis up with a firm and strict tenderness, never dreaming of sparing him the excessive hardships of the discipline of those days, to which he submitted with great humility.

"God, in Whom he trusted," said Joinville, "watched over him from childhood to the end, and particularly in childhood, when he greatly needed guidance. . . . As for his soul, God guided it through the good teaching of the mother who taught him to believe in God and to love Him, and who surrounded him with pious persons. And, child as he was, she made him hear and repeat all the Hours and listen to sermons on festivals. He remembered that his mother had often given him to understand that she would rather he were dead than that he should commit a mortal sin."

"The youth of Monseigneur St Louis," says

Queen Margaret's confessor, "was not spent in vain, but he passed it in a very saintly manner. When he was about fourteen, he was still under the guardianship of the noble lady his mother, Queen Blanche, whom he obeyed in all things. She caused him to be carefully educated and herself watched over him. She made him go about in grand and noble attire, such as befitted a great king. At that time he occasionally went a-hunting, or on the river, or indulged in pastimes of that character, such as were seemly and proper. His master was, however, always with him, teaching and instructing him in letters, and as the pious king himself admitted, this master did not fail to chastise him at times for 'disciplinary reason.' And at that time the king heard Mass and Vespers daily, and all the Canonical Hours, and that did not prevent him from saying them privately with another. He avoided all improper games and kept himself from all unseemly or dishonourable things. He injured no one by word or deed, and always addressed those to whom he spoke with respect."

Louis IX. was then an amiable child, of a fine countenance, with fair hair, like the members of the House of Hainault, to which he was allied through his grandmother Isabella, mother of Louis VIII.; he was serious and affable, attentive and thoughtful; already firm and patient, prudent and moderate, but above all, pious and profoundly Christian in heart and mind. From his earliest age, Blanche had taught him the habit of alms-giving, which she herself practised to a very high degree. There is a charming anecdote bearing on this subject, contained in the sermon of a contemporary of the holy king. "King Louis of France, the present monarch," says Stephen of Bourbon, "once said an excellent thing which was repeated to me by a monk who was present on the occasion and heard it himself. One morning, when he was quite young, a number of beggars were waiting for alms in the courtyard of the Palace. At an early hour, while everyone else was still sleeping, he came out of his chamber dressed as a simple squire, and accompanied by only one servant bearing a large sum in small coins; these he began to distribute with his own hands, giving amply to those who seemed to him most needy. As he was returning to his rooms he was met by a monk who had observed the scene through a window, where he was in conversation with the king's mother, who said, 'Sire, I have watched your misdeeds.' 'My dear brother,' replied the prince in confusion, 'those people are my retainers; they fight for me (by their prayers) against all adversaries, and maintain peace in the kingdom. I have not yet paid them the salary due to them.'"

This certainly is a fair beginning of a royal life. We need not, however, believe that the young prince had, at that early age, arrived at the high degree of perfection to which he attained later, and that Christian education had to combat no taint of original sin; that the heroic virtue of his will had to fight against and triumph over no natural tendencies to evil. It is little likely that this could have been the case, and if only in vindication of the zealous preceptor who from time to time roughly corrected him for "disciplinary reasons," we may think that his pious biographers have occasionally, actuated by a very natural inclination, carried back to his childhood the moral perfection as well as the outward habits of his maturity. M. Langlois, profiting by his privileges as historian and critic, took an opposite view to theirs and adopted, while arriving at the same conclusion, the somewhat thankless task of "Devil's advocate"; and we must not fear to follow him, according to our own opinions, in this path of examination and retrospective research.

It would perhaps be going too far, and outstepping the reality of our knowledge concerning St Louis, to affirm as an undoubted fact the "violence of his temper," even though adding "that he often succeeded in mastering it." But we may admit that he inherited from his father and mother a certain sensitiveness and quickness of temper with a tendency to anger, especially when convinced that he was right. It is certain that Blanche was anything but meek and gentle when offended, and that on the contrary, there was something proud and overbearing in her nature. As for Louis VIII., his contemporaries remarked that he was not easily put out, but when once angry was very hard to appease. At all events, St Louis brought this hereditary tendency under the strait yoke of justice and the most exacting charity, as has been proved by thousands of acts on record. We may find some trace of this natural inclination, and of the triumph of his will, in a charming story told by Joinville, the friend and biographer of the holy king, who though early convinced of and almost penetrated with his saintliness, yet had no scruples in seizing and noting with a certain curiosity and amusement, the human, not to say the defective traits of his character.

"While the king was fortifying Cæsarea, I went to see him in his tent. He was speaking to the Legate, and as soon as he saw me enter the room he rose, drew me aside and said, 'You know I only retained you until Easter, so please tell me what I am to give you in order that you may remain with me for a year from Easter.' And I told him that I did not want him to give me more of his money than he then paid me, but that I would make another bargain with him.

"'Since,' said I, 'you get angry when you are asked for anything, I want your promise that you will not be angry during the whole of this year when I ask you for anything; and if you refuse me, I, on my side, will not get angry.' When he heard that he burst out laughing, and said he would keep me on those conditions; then he took me by the hand and led me before the Legate and his Council and told them of our bargain, and they were all glad of it, for I was the richest man in the camp."

Some time after this, a knight was sent away from the camp for misconduct, and his arms and horse were confiscated. "I went to beg the king," says Joinville, "to give me the horse for a poor gentleman in the camp. The king replied that my demand was unreasonable, for the horse was worth eighty *livres*. And I answered, 'How can you violate our agreement by being angry at my request.' At which he laughingly said, 'You may say what you like, I will not be angry.' However, I did not get the horse for the poor gentleman after all."

But beyond anger, or rather irritability, we can recognise easily in the natural character of St Louis, elevated and perfected though it was by the submission of his will to Grace, a somewhat strong tendency to obstinacy, the natural outcome of an excess of that royal and beautiful quality of firmness which he had inherited from his mother. It is not perhaps too rash to interpret in this sense the following story also told by Joinville.

"When we had been ten days at sea (returning from the Crusade), we came to a port situated about two leagues from a castle called Hyères, belonging to the Count of Provence, who was afterwards king of Sicily. The queen and the whole council were of opinion that the king should land there, since the place belonged to his brother. The king replied that he would not leave his vessel till it reached Aigues-Mortes, in his own land. He kept us there the whole of Wednesday and Thursday, and we were unable to persuade him.

"On these Marseilles vessels there are two helms which are so wonderfully attached to two bars that the vessel can be turned to right or left as quickly as one can turn a horse. On Friday the king was sitting on one of these rudder-bars, when he called me and said, 'Seneschal, what do you think of this matter?' And I said, 'Sire, it would only be just if the same thing happened to you as to Madame de

Bourbon, who refused to land here, but put out to sea again to reach Aigues-Mortes, and was seven weeks at sea.'

"Then the king called his council and told them what I had said, and asked them what they would advise. They all agreed that he should land, for he would not be acting wisely if he again put his own person, his wife and children in danger on sea, when once he was safe. The king yielded to the advice we gave, much to the joy of the queen (Margaret)."

Whatever may have been the original imperfections of St Louis, it is certain that the education he received from Blanche of Castile was an efficacious remedy and an increasing help in the development of his innate qualities. The ever-present memory of his obligations towards her, not only as a king but also as a man, strengthened his filial love to such a point as to keep him ever in a spirit of docility, not childish, but reasonable, and even to induce him to accept the somewhat heavy burden of certain susceptibilities of Blanche, who, although a model mother, was not, as we shall see, a model mother-in-law. When he heard the news of the death of her to whom he owed so much, Louis' grief was terrible, though always Christian.

"The news of his mother's death reached the king at Sayette (at Jaffa, according to Geoffrey of Baulieu). He showed such deep grief that no one could speak with him for two days. After that he sent a servant to summon me. When I came to him in his chamber, where he was alone, and when he saw me, he stretched out his arms and said, 'Ah, Seneschal, I have lost my mother.'

"'Sire, I am not surprised,' said I, 'for she had to die. But I am surprised that you, who are wise, should show such deep grief; for you know the wise man has said that however sad a man's heart may be, it should not appear on his face, for a man who shows his sorrow makes his enemies joyful and grieves his friends.'"

It is difficult not to find this remark of Joinville's somewhat out of place; but from being lectured, as he often was in a friendly manner by St Louis, it seems that he had the habit of lecturing in his turn, though with less right. Geoffrey of Baulieu shows truer sentiment and fuller information regarding this matter.

"While the king remained at Jaffa to repair the walls of the town, news was brought to him of the saintly death of Madame Blanche, his very august mother. As soon as Monseigneur the Legate received this information, he took with him the Archbishop of Tyre, who was then the king's seal-bearer, and they were also pleased to take me as a third. Then the Legate went to the king, and we with him, and he asked the king to grant him a private audience in his chamber in our presence. Remarking the Legate's serious manner, the king immediately concluded that he had some grave news to communicate. Being a man filled with the thought of God, he led us, with the Legate, to the chapel which opened out of his chamber; then having caused the door of his chamber to be closed, he sat with us before the altar. The

THE MAN 13

Legate then wisely reminded the king of the great and numberless blessings he had received from the divine goodness since early childhood, and, above all, of the great blessing God had given him in the mother who had brought him up in such a Christian manner, and had conducted and administered the affairs of his kingdom with such faithfulness and wisdom. After a short silence, he told him with sighs and tears of the sad and deplorable event which had occurred in the death of the queen. The king first cried aloud, then wept; then he knelt before the altar, and joining his hands said, very piously and still weeping, 'I thank Thee, Lord, my God, for having lent me, so long as it seemed good unto Thee, Madame, my well-beloved mother; and now, according to Thy good pleasure, Thou hast called her away by bodily death. It is true, Lord, that I loved her above all other mortal creatures, and that she well deserved such love; but since such is Thy will, may Thy holy Name be praised, for ever and ever, Amen.'

"Then when the Legate had said a brief commendatory prayer for the soul of the dead, the king desired to remain alone with me in his chapel. The Legate and the Archbishop retired, and the king remained some time before the altar in pious meditation, mingled with sighs. But, fearing he might be worn out by such excessive sorrow, I drew near to try and console him, in so far as it was in my power, and I told him humbly that now he had rendered unto nature that which was due unto nature, and that it was time also to yield to the grace of God in him, that which was seemly from reason illuminated by grace. He received this advice wisely, and resolved to follow it. Soon, indeed, he left his chapel and retired to his oratory, where he usually said the Hours privately. He took me there alone with him, and, as he wished it, we said together the whole Office for the dead, that is to say, Vespers and the Vigils, with the nine lessons. And it was no slight cause of admiration to me to note that, though his heart had been so recently and cruelly wounded, I could not, so far as I remember, notice that he made any omission or error in reciting a single verse or lesson, as generally occurs when the human heart has been overwhelmed by sudden or grievous news. This I attributed to the power of divine grace, and to the constancy of his heart. He showed himself a faithful son to the soul of his pious mother, for he asked for a great number of Masses on her behalf, and the repetition of numerous prayers in religious communities. Personally he attended henceforth a daily Mass specially said for his mother."

CHAPTER II

THE HUSBAND—MARGARET OF PROVENCE

ST LOUIS'S marriage was, like his education, the work of Blanche of Castile. He was nineteen years old when, in 1233, his mother took steps to find him a wife. Her choice fell upon the Princess Margaret, eldest daughter of Raimond Berenger, Count of Provence. Politics, no doubt, had great weight in this choice, as was inevitable. But Blanche had not omitted to gain information regarding the personal qualities of the girl, who was beautiful, pious, and thoroughly educated by her father. The negotiation was not difficult. Raimond Berenger hastened to accept the proposal made to him.

"Gautier Cornu, archbishop of Sens, and Jean of Nesle," says M. Elie Berger from contemporary authors and documents, "went to Provence to fetch the young princess, who came to the court accompanied by her uncle William, bishop elect of Valence. She had, no doubt, a numerous suite; at all events the royal accounts mentioned on this occasion a minstrel of the Count of Provence and six trumpeters, who came with Margaret. On her journey to Sens, the king's betrothed stopped, on the 19th May, at the Abbey of Tournus. At the same time Louis IX. came from Paris by Fontainebleau, Pont-sur-Yonne, and the Abbey of Sainte Colombe, near Sens. He had with him his mother, his brothers, Robert and Alphonse, his cousin, Alphonse of Portugal, a nephew of Blanche, who was brought up with the young princes. Blanche of Castile's other children, Isabella and Charles, had remained in Paris. Besides the ladies of her household, the queen certainly had with her a very great number of officers and noblemen; the High Chamberlain of France, Barthelemy de Roye, Chamberlain Jean de Beaumont, Ferry Pâtè, subsequently Marshal, are mentioned in connection with the king's marriage in the household accounts, as are also Raimond of Toulouse, and the Countess Jeanne of Flanders. The queen had hired boats and horses, according to custom, to transport all her people.

"The court remained at Sens from the 26th to 28th May 1234, and the wedding was probably solemnised on the 27th. At any rate, on that day Louis IX. settled Margaret's dower by a document in which he speaks of her as already his wife. Although at that time the expenses of the royal household were in no way exorbitant, Blanche and her son exhibited on this solemn occasion a fitting splendour; the household accounts speak of the golden crown which was made for the young queen, a 'gold bonnet' repaired for her use, two spoons and a gold goblet, certainly intended for the royal table; the goblet was afterwards given to the Cupbearer of France. The king's crown was put

THE MAN

into good condition, and jewels were bought from the Countess of Flanders' goldsmith.

"Time would fail to tell all the garments, bedding, and articles of all kinds which Blanche of Castile had purchased for her son's marriage; the robes ordered for the king, those which were intended for the officers and the noblemen of the Court, for Prince Robert, for Prince Alfonse, for their cousin the Prince of Portugal, for the Count of Toulouse; the furs brought for the young queen or given to the ladies of the court. Among the robes distributed for the coronation many were of silk and many of purple cloth; some were given according to custom to those who were knighted on the occasion of the royal wedding. The queen had had lodgings prepared for the court at Sens, and by her order a house had been retained for the Countess of Flanders. The town was unable to accommodate all those who had accompanied the king, but tents had been brought. They put up, moreover, a house of branches, a 'feuillée,' the object of which is not indicated by the accounts, containing the throne covered with silk for the use of the king. Perhaps there the minstrels were heard, many of whom belonged to the Prince Robert's suite. Finally, scaffoldings were erected in front of the church of Saint Etienne, where the coronation of Margaret was to take place.

"Many gentlemen of the court had been sent before the princess; when she drew near the king, Blanche and the princes went to meet her. The day after the wedding, the young queen was crowned by the

Archbishop of Sens who anointed her with the holy oil. . . . Charity was not forgotten in the midst of these rejoicings; the sick were brought to the king who ordered that money should be distributed to them; a poor man whose horse had been killed during the festivities received compensation. The court started for Paris, probably on May 29th, by Montereau-faut-Yonne and Fontainebleau. Margaret had received as dower the town of Mans and its appurtenances, with Mortagne and Mauves-sur-Huisne. Her marriage settlement was ten thousand marks, a very large sum, which was perhaps never entirely paid, for we see that in 1266 eight thousand marks were still due to St Louis in connection with his marriage."

The lively, tender and constant affection of St Louis for Margaret, who reciprocated it, is one of the most characteristic and charming traits of his life. We learn from the naïvely exact reports of pious witnesses of his virtues, how, from the beginning, day by day more deeply penetrated by grace, he was able to reconcile the warmth of this conjugal love with the deep sense and ascetic practice of Christian chastity, which was one of the dominant traits of his nature. Without being altogether a saint herself, the young queen showed herself worthy of this affection of a saint. Their common fondness suffered from the stern and in this case somewhat jealous character of Blanche of Castile, but for this very reason it stands out in our eyes as a pleasant contrast to the harshness of the queen-mother in the account which we owe to Joinville.

THE MAN

The death of Blanche, whom the good seneschal (perhaps because as a great lord he felt a certain amount of sympathy for the feudal and aristocratic party which she had fought and conquered) does not appear to have greatly loved or mourned, gave him an opportunity of finding room in his book for those small feminine bickerings which, as we see, are to be found in the most exemplary families.

"Madame Marie de Vertus," says he, "a very good lady and a very holy woman, came to tell me that the queen (Margaret) showed great grief, and begged me to go and comfort her. And when I came there, I found her weeping; and I told her that he spake truth who said that we should not believe in women, for it was the woman you hated the most who is dead, and you now show such deep grief. And she told me that it was not for the queen (Blanche) that she wept, but for the king's sorrow and the grief which he showed, and for her daughter (who since then became queen of Navarre) who had remained in the care of men.

"The harshness which Queen Blanche showed to Queen Margaret was such, that Queen Blanche would not allow her son to remain in his wife's company, if she could prevent it, except in the evening when he retired with her. The house in which the king and queen liked best to live was at Pontoise, because the king's room was above and the queen's room below.

"And they had so arranged matters that they held converse on a winding staircase which led from one room to the other. And they had so settled matters that when the ushers saw the queen coming into the chamber of the king, her son, they rapped the door with their wands, and the king came running into his chamber, so that his mother should find him there; and thus in their turn did the ushers of the Queen Margaret's chamber when the Queen Blanche was going there, so that she might find the Queen Margaret.

"Once the king was with his wife, and she was in danger of death, being ill after the birth of a child. The Queen Blanche came there, took her son by the hand and said, 'Come away, you have no business here.' When Queen Margaret saw that the mother was leading the king away, she cried out: 'Alas! You will not let me see my lord either in life or death'; and then she swooned, and they thought she was dead. The king, who thought she was dying, returned, and it was with great trouble that she was brought to herself again."

The behaviour of Margaret of Provence at Damietta, during the disasters of the Egyptian crusade, gives us a high conception of the qualities of this princess, which is fixed as a living picture on our minds by the expressive and simple pen of Joinville.

"Now you have heard already of the great persecutions which the king and we suffered; the queen did not escape these persecutions, as you will learn hereafter. For, three days before she lay in, the news of the king's capture reached her, and she was so alarmed by this news that every time she fell asleep in her bed, it seemed to her that all her chamber was full of Saracens, and she cried out: 'Help! Help!'

And, fearing that the child she bare would die, she made an old knight, eighty years old, sleep by her bed, and he held her hand. Each time the queen cried out, he said, 'Madame, be not afraid, for I am here.'

"Before she was delivered she made everyone leave her room except this knight, and knelt before him, asking him a favour, and the knight granted it to her on oath. And she said to him, 'I beg you,' says she, 'by the promise you have given, that if the Saracens take this town, you will cut my head off rather than let them take me.' And the knight replied, 'Rest assured that I will do so willingly, for I had already thought that I would kill you before they captured us.'

"The queen bare a son who was named John, and they called him Tristan, because of the great sorrow at the time he was born. The very day that she lay in, she was told that those of Pisa and Genoa and the other communes, wanted to retreat. The day after she lay in, she called them all around her bed, so that the room was quite full, and she said to them: 'My lords, for the love of God, do not leave this town, for you see that my lord the king would be lost, and all those who are prisoners, if the town were lost. And if this does not touch you, take pity on the weak creature lying here, and so wait until I can rise.' And they replied, 'Madame, what shall we do? For we are dying of hunger in this town.' And she told them that they must not go away because of famine; 'for I will have all the provisions in this town bought up, and I will retain you all from this moment at the king's expense.' They consulted together, and came back to her and told her that they would willingly remain, and the queen (whom may God pardon) had all the provisions of the town bought in, which cost her three hundred and sixty thousand livres, and over. She was obliged to leave her bed before the fitting time, because the city had to be given up to the Saracens. The queen came to Acre to await the king."

Margaret of Provence, though a courageous and devoted wife, had not the genius and strong political insight of Blanche of Castile. The glimpses we have of the capabilities she would have shown in the management of serious affairs, had she been trusted with such management, seem to indicate a character not entirely free from passion and too accessible to the influence of affection, personal interest and animosity. The rivalry which arose between her and Charles of Anjou, her brother-in-law, regarding the inheritance of Provence, after the death of the Count Raymond Berenger, was a cause of anxiety to St Louis, who tried in vain to reconcile his wife and brother. At least the fault was not all on the side of Margaret in this case, while it is difficult to find any excuse for the engagement into which she made her son, Prince Philip, the heir to the throne, enter under oath and without her husband's knowledge. In view of his eventual accession to the crown, he promised his mother that he would remain under her guardianship until the age of thirty; that he would take no counsellor whom she might not approve; that he would enter into no alliance with Charles of Anjou; that he would tell her of any machinations which he might learn of against her; that he would not make any grants beyond a certain sum. But a Bull of Urban IV., which St Louis probably asked for when he gained knowledge of this singular agreement, freed the young Prince from this rash oath (6th July 1263).

Persuaded, no doubt, that the authority which he entrusted to Blanche, even after he had taken actual possession of the government, could only be exceptionally justified by unequalled talents and services, Louis only allowed Margaret to exercise a somewhat restricted and always subordinate influence in political matters, without, however, limiting her absolutely to the performance of her family duties. Moreover, when he started for his second crusade, although this time she remained in France, he did not think well to confide to her the reins of government, but left the regency to Mathieu of Vendôme, Abbot of Sainte-Dennis, and to Simon, Count of Nesle. Even in private affairs, in spite of his great affection, he insisted on respect being paid not only to his liberty but also to his marital authority. One of St Louis's most recent historians has thought it not unlikely that some slight discussion with Margaret gave rise to, or at any rate were alluded to in, the amusing conversation between husband and wife which the pious King related one day to Robert of Sorbon, one of his intimate friends, and the latter in his turn relates to us as follows:—

"A prince, whom I shall not name, used to dress

very simply; and that habit displeased his wife very much, for she liked pomp and ostentation, and she was constantly complaining about him to her family. At last the husband, tired of her reproaches, said, 'Madame, would you be pleased if I covered myself with costly garments?' 'Yes, certainly, and I want you to do so.' 'Well, I agree, and am ready to please you, for the law of marriage requires that the husband should seek to please his wife. Only this obligation is reciprocal; you will, therefore, be obliged to conform to my wish.' 'And what is that wish?' 'It is that you should wear the most humble costume; you will take mine, and I yours' (we know that in those times men's garments differed little from those of the women). The princess, as may be supposed, was deaf to that offer, and abstained henceforth from raising the question."

Joinville learnt one day from Margaret herself that the king did not allow her to bind herself, even towards God, without his knowledge. Here again the vivid memory and the brilliant pen of the good seneschal seem to bring back to life for us the amiable queen, who was after all (and what praise can be higher) the worthy consort of St Louis.

"The wind rose so high and was so rough that it was driving us with great force towards the island of Cyprus. The sailors threw their anchors out against the wind, and were unable to stop the vessel until they had cast five. It was necessary to knock down the partitions of the king's chamber, and no one inside dared to remain there for fear that the wind would carry them into the sea. At that moment the Constable of France, Monseigneur Gilles Le Brun, and I were sleeping in the king's chamber; and at that moment the queen opened the door of the chamber, thinking to find the king within.

"And I asked her what she had come to seek. She said she had come to speak to the king for him to promise some pilgrimage to God, or to His saints, by which God would deliver us from the danger in which we were, for the sailors had said that we were in peril of drowning. And I said to her, 'Madame, promise a journey to Monseigneur St Nicholas of Varangeville, and I will undertake for him that God will bring you safe back to France, with the king and your children.' 'Seneschal,' said she, 'truly I would do so willingly, but the king is so peculiar that if he knew I had promised without his consent, he would never allow me to go.'

"'You will do one thing, if God brings you back to France, you will promise him a ship in silver, worth five marks, for the king, for you, and for your three children; and I warrant you that God will bring you back to France, for I promised St Nicholas that if he saved us from the danger in which we were during the night,[1] I would go on foot and without shoes from Joinville to pray to him.' And she told me that she would promise St Nicholas the silver ship, and told me to be her warrant; and I told her I would willingly do so. She went away and tarried only a short while, then she came to us and said to me, 'St

[1] The previous night the ship had hit against a sand-bank, and had been in great danger of complete shipwreck.

Nicholas has preserved us from this danger, for the wind has fallen.'

"When the queen (whom may God pardon) had returned to France, she had the silver ship made in Paris; and on the ship were the king, the queen and the three children, all in silver; the sailor, the mast, the helm and ropes, all in silver; and the sails all sewn in silver thread. And the queen said the making had cost a hundred livres. When the ship was ready, the queen sent it to me at Joinville to have it taken to St Nicholas, and I did this; and I saw it still at St Nicholas when we escorted the king's sister to Haguenau, to the King of Germany."

There was an important circumstance in the life and the reign of her husband, when Margaret, in her turn using her right, fortunately made her will prevail. This was when St Louis, seeing his son had reached an age at which he might reign, secretly told the queen of his intention to become a Religious (this was perhaps the first origin of the above mentioned agreement), and asked her to acquiesce in his pious intention. Margaret refused her consent, and, far from yielding to his persuasions, she strongly put forward all the arguments which should retain him on the throne.

CHAPTER III

THE FATHER AND THE BROTHER—THE PRINCES AND PRINCESSES OF THE BLOOD

QUEEN MARGARET, whose life was prolonged to a somewhat advanced age (she died during the reign of her grandson, Philip the Fair, on the 21st December 1295), bore her husband no less than eleven children. The eldest of her sons, Louis, a prince of great promise, died during his father's lifetime at the age of sixteen. To him the pious king, lying seriously ill at Fontainebleau (April 1258), said these beautiful words: "Fair son, I pray you to make the people of your kingdom love you, for truly, I would rather a Scotchman came from Scotland to govern the people of the kingdom well and loyally than that you should govern them badly in the sight of all."

The presumptive succession passed to Prince Philip, only fourteen months younger than his brother, who reigned under the name of Philip III. with the surname of Philip the Bold. Putting aside the children who died at an early age, the other princes were:—Jean-Tristan, born at Damietta during the disasters of the Egyptian Crusade, who married Yolande of Burgundy, Countess of Nevers, and died without issue shortly before his father on

August 3rd, 1270, during the Tunisian Crusade; Peter, Count of Alençon, married to Jeanne of Châtillon, Countess of Blois and of Chartres, who died in 1283 without issue; Robert, Count of Clermont in Beauvoisis, who was the husband of Beatrice of Burgundy, Lady of Bourbon, and became, owing to this marriage, the stem of the ducal house of Bourbon which was, three centuries later, to wear the crown of St Louis in the person of Henri IV. as a descendant of Robert. The princesses were Isabella, married to Thibault II., Count of Champagne, King of Navarre; Blanche, who married Ferdinand, hereditary Prince of Castile; Margaret, who was given in marriage to John, Duke of Brabant, and Agnes, wife of Robert II., Duke of Burgundy.

From a temporal point of view, St Louis showed all the solicitude of a loving father towards his children, as may be seen by the appanages with which he provided them and the brilliant alliances which he secured for them. It has been remarked, in this connection, that they all remained in the world. He had, however, greatly desired that his daughter Isabella should become a nun, and had even especially exhorted her to do so. With the same intention he had his daughter Blanche educated at the Abbey of Maubuisson. He had also cherished the hope of seeing his sons John and Peter devote themselves to the service of God in the two orders which he most encouraged, the Dominicans and the Franciscans; and to suggest the thought to them, he had even ordered almost from their birth that their education should be entrusted to the Jacobins and the Cordeliers of Paris, where he wished them to reside as soon as they reached the age of reason. But as his pious hopes were not realised, he knew how to respect the legitimate freedom of his children in a just and Christian manner, far from allowing himself to be carried by his zeal beyond the limits of his authority as king and father.

But for their Christian education and the spiritual advancement of their souls, he exercised fully by authority or by persuasion his paternal rights and duties. Not content with choosing their masters, he also instructed them himself. "Before he lay down in his bed," Joinville tells us, "he made his children come around him and told them the deeds of good kings and emperors, and that they should take example by such good men. And he also told them the deeds of bad princes who, by their luxury, rapine and avarice, had lost their kingdoms. 'And I remind you of these things,' said he, 'that you may avoid them, so that God be not wroth against you.' He made them learn the Hours of Our Lady, and made them say the daily Hours before him, to accustom them to hear the Hours when they should govern their lands."

Above all, he preached to them by example, by associating them with his good works, and even with some practices which we may almost call excessive. When the Hospital of Compiègne, which he had built, was ready to receive the sick, "the saintly king on the one hand," says Queen Margaret's confessor, "and Monseigneur Thibaut, his son-in-law, and the king of Navarre, who assisted him, on the other hand, carried on a silken sheet the first poor patient who was put in the newly built hospital, and put him on a newly made bed, and left the silken sheet in which they had carried him over him; and that same day Monseigneur Louis, then the eldest son of St Louis, and Philip, who was after him the noble king of France, also carried the second patient into the said hospital and put him in a second bed, and thus did also some other barons who were there with him."

He was strict as to the obedience which he considered that his children owed him in his double character of father and of king. This is proved by the good seneschal of Champagne in the following quaint anecdote. "After these things, my lord the king called my lord Philip his son, the father of the present king (Philip the Fair), and the king Thibaut, and sat down at the entrance to his oratory, and putting a hand on the ground, said, ' Sit down here quite close to me, so that we may not be overheard,' ' Ah, Sire,' said they, ' we should not presume to sit so near to you.' And he said to me, ' Seneschal, sit down here.' And thus did I, and so near to him that my robe touched his. And he made them sit down beyond me, and said to them, ' You did wrong truly, you who are my sons, and who did not at once do what I commanded you; be careful this does not happen again.' And they said they would not do it again."

Isabella of France, queen of Navarre, Thibaut's wife, was St Louis's favourite daughter. He could not prevail on her to embrace the monastic life, but in the high rank assured by her marriage she retained the sentiments and gave herself up to the practice of most fervent piety. The saintly king, who knew her spirit of faith and penitence, did not hesitate on one occasion to give her a present which, even then, would doubtless not have been appreciated by all princesses. "The pious king," says Queen Margaret's confessor, "sent to his daughter of Navarre two or three ivory boxes, and at the bottom of those boxes there was a little iron nail, to which he had attached small iron chains of an ell long or thereabouts; these chains were enclosed in each of the boxes, and the said Queen of Navarre would discipline and scourge herself with them sometimes, as she told her confessor when she was nearing death. And the pious king sent moreover to his same daughter a horsehair belt as wide as the palm of a man's hand, with which she girded herself occasionally, as she told her confessor at the same time. And with all that the pious king sent to the said queen a letter written with his own hand, in which it was stated that he was sending her by Brother John of Mons, of the order of Friars Minor (then the confessor of that queen and sometimes of the pious king), a discipline contained in each of the boxes, as is said above, and he begged her in that letter often to use these disciplines for her own sins and for the sins of her poor father."

His affection for Isabella caused him to send her, in the form of a letter, some *Instructions* written with his own hand, and he also composed some with still greater care, for the prince Philip, heir to his crown;

a double monument which reflects with matchless fidelity the soul of the saintly king. In a considerable portion of their contents, these two precious documents are, as is natural, conceived in analogous and sometimes almost identical terms. But there are also to be found special counsels, as was fitting, appropriate to the different circumstances of either pupil. As for instance the counsel to Isabella: "Dear daughter, obey humbly your husband, and your father and mother, in such things as are agreeable to God; you must willingly render unto each one of them that which is due, because of the love which you must feel for them; and, moreover, you must do it still more for the love of our Lord who has so ordered it; but against God you must obey no one. Dear daughter, take such pains to become perfect in all good things that you may be an example to those who see you and hear about you. Me seems it good that you should not have too great a number of robes and jewels, in accordance with the position you occupy, but I think it would be better used for giving alms, at any rate with that which would be superfluous; and I think it would be good for you not to spend too much time on decking and adorning yourself; and be careful not to be extravagant in your dress, but in that be rather inclined to do too little than too much."

Among the counsels given to Philip to which we shall have many occasions of referring, we will at the present moment only note this one: "Love your brothers and always desire their happiness and advancement; take the place of a father towards them to teach them all good. But beware, however great your affection for any man, lest you should swerve from strict justice and do aught to another which you should not do." Such, indeed, has been St Louis's conduct towards the noble group of princes his younger brothers, who had, like him, received the stamp of a wise education and profited by the vigilant care of the queen mother. "The members of the royal family," says M. Elie Berger, "lived together, and Blanche of Castile took charge of them. In the midst of most important business she always remained the mother of the family, just as Louis IX., king of France, never ceased to be the eldest brother."

The first of St Louis's younger brothers, Prince Robert, born in 1216, to whom Louis VIII. had bequeathed in his will the County of Artois as appanage, was married in 1237 to Matilda, daughter of Henri II., Duke of Brabant. He was the most brilliant but the least wise scion of this noble house. From his youth he had manifested a taste for luxury, fine armour and beautiful horses. The chivalrous courage with which he was gifted, had something wild and reckless in it. His fiery valour cost him his life, and was the cause of a serious loss suffered by the advance-guard of the Christian army on the day of the battle of Mansourah (8th February 1250). His affectionate nature had rendered him peculiarly dear to St Louis, to whom the news of his death was a cruel blow. "Then came brother Henri de Ronnay, Provost of the Hospital, and he kissed the armed hand of the king, who had crossed the river.

And the king asked if he had any news of his brother, the Count of Artois; and he said that he truly had some news, for it was certain that his brother the Count of Artois was in Paradise. 'Ah, Sire,' said the Provost, 'be comforted, for to no other king of France has such great honour come as to you. For, to fight your enemies, you have crossed a river, swimming, have disconcerted and driven them from the battle-field, and taken their weapons and tents, in which you will sleep again this night.' And the king replied that God be praised for all that He had given him; and then very large tears fell from his eyes."

Alphonse of France, born on the 11th November 1220, had inherited the County of Poitou by his father's will. The energetic and able policy of Blanche of Castile procured him the County of Toulouse, through his marriage with Jeanne, daughter of Raymond VII., as was stipulated by the Treaty of Paris 1229 and accomplished later. The festivities held at Saumur by Louis in June 1241, on the occasion of the majority of his brother, upon whom he had just conferred the honour of knighthood, gave Joinville, who was present, an opportunity of tracing a living picture.

"The king held high court at Saumur in Anjou, and I was there, and I assure you that it was the best ordered I have ever seen. For there ate at the king's table, by his side, the Count of Poitiers, whom he had knighted on St John's day; and beyond the Count of Poitiers ate the Count John of Dreux, whom he had also newly made a knight;

beyond the Count of Dreux ate the Count de la Marche; and beyond the Count de la Marche the good Count Peter of Bretagne. And in front of the king's table, opposite the Count of Dreux, ate my lord the King of Navarre, in tunic and satin cloak, decorated with a belt, a buckle, and a golden cap; and I carved before him. The Count of Artois, his brother, served before the king; before the king, the good Count John of Soissons carved. To guard the king's table there were my lord Imbert of Beaujeu, who since became Constable of France, and my lord Enguerrand of Coucy and my lord Archambaud of Bourbon. Behind these three barons there were full thirty of their knights, in tunics of silk cloth, to guard them; and behind these knights there were a great number of sergeants, bearing the arms of the Count of Poitiers embroidered in silk. The king was dressed in a blue satin tunic and on his head a cotton cap, which suited him ill, for he was then a young man."

Of all the sons of Queen Blanche, Alphonse of Poitiers was, after or with St Louis, the one who took most after her in uprightness of mind and administrative qualities. Without being a saint like his brother, he was one of the wisest princes and most clever administrators of his day. And the king, whom he rarely left, for he governed his lands with the greatest personal care, but by correspondence and from a distance, added great esteem and confidence to the affection he felt for him. When St Louis set out for the Crusade to Egypt, whither Alphonse was to accompany him, he allowed the latter to put off his departure for a year, not merely to comfort Blanche of Castile's maternal heart, but to assist the Regent; for the presence of this prince was a great assistance to her in her heavy task, and she could not have a "counsellor more worthy to second her." So, when the king resolved to lengthen his stay in the East, he sent the Count of Poitiers back to France with Charles of Anjou, his youngest brother, to assist Blanche in the government of the kingdom; and after the death of their mother these two brothers of the king really governed the kingdom until his return, under the name of the Prince Louis, then heir to the throne. "Alphonse presided over the council in which affairs were discussed." Nevertheless, St Louis took him with him on his Crusade to Tunis, and he died on the return, 21st August 1271, without issue.

Charles of Anjou was with reason associated with his brother Alphonse in the marks of high esteem shewn them by St Louis. He was indeed a most remarkable man. Born in March 1226, endowed in 1246 with the Counties of Anjou and Maine, his marriage (31st January 1246) with Beatrice, younger sister of Queen Margaret, brought him the County of Provence. Invested by Pope Clement IV. (28th June 1265) with the kingdom of Naples and Sicily, he conquered it in combat with Manfred, natural son of the Emperor Frederick II. To this he added later the acquisition of eventual rights to the kingdom of Jerusalem, and he did not hesitate to extend his views to the empire of Constantinople. Fully conscious of his rare political and military qualities, he gave himself up, as is evident, without scruple to the intense impulse of a strong and grasping ambition. More bold and enterprising but less wise than Alphonse, he remained far inferior to St Louis in holiness. The intellectual and moral traits of Blanche of Castile were so accentuated in him as to become defects. An ardent and sincere believer, a zealous Christian possessed of strong piety and admirable purity of morals, his austerity was not prepossessing, and his firmness, always harsh and imperious, occasionally became unjust and cruel. "Charles," says the Italian historian Villani, "was wise in council and brave in battle. He spoke little and hardly ever laughed. He was chaste as a monk and a good Catholic. His justice was stern, his glance betokened pride. He slept little. He was generous to his knights, but greedy of acquiring lands, lordships, money, wherever it might come from, to supply him in his enterprises and his wars. He despised courtiers, minstrels, and singers." During his last years his character was still more sobered by the disaster of the Sicilian Vespers, and by other reverses not altogether unmerited. He died at the Castle of Foggia in Capitanate, on Sunday the 7th January 1295.

Considering the character of Charles of Anjou, it is not surprising that St Louis had to put into special practice when dealing with him, the unswerving justice which he recommended to his son Philip. He did not, as we shall see, sacrifice to his brotherly affection any of the rights of equity or of royal authority. He had also conformed himself beforehand to the advice, "to take the place of a

father towards his brothers, to teach them all good."
He associated them, as he did his children, with all
his good works, and did not fail, even in ordinary
matters of conduct, to warn and admonish them.
"While a wall was being built at the Abbey of
Royaumont," says Queen Margaret's confessor,
"the pious king, who was then living in his castle
of Asnières, not far from the said abbey, often came
there to hear Mass and the other offices, and to visit
the place; and as the monks, in accordance with the
custom of the Cistercian order, after Terce came to
begin work and to carry stones and mortar to the
place where the said wall was building, the pious
king took the hand-barrow and carried it loaded
with stones, and went in front and a monk carried it
behind. And thus did the pious king several times at
the aforesaid period; and also at that time the pious
king made his brothers, my lord Robert, my lord
Alphonse, and my lord Charles carry the hand-
barrow, and with each of them there was one of
the aforesaid monks to carry one end of the hand-
barrow, and the saintly king made other knights of
his company do the same. And because his brothers
sometimes wanted to speak, and shout and play, the
pious king said to them, 'The monks are now
keeping silence, and so should we.' And as the
brothers of the pious king, having heavily loaded
their hand-barrows, wanted to rest on the way
before reaching the wall, he said to them, 'The
monks do not rest, neither should you rest.'"

One day his reproach was sterner on board the ship
which, after the disaster and captivity in Egypt, was

taking the king and his brothers to Syria. "During six days," says Joinville, "while we were at sea, I being ill, always sat near the king. And he told me how he had been captured and how he had negotiated his ransom and ours, with the help of God. And he made me relate how I had been captured on the water, and after that, he told me how I ought to be very grateful to our Lord since He had delivered me from such great peril. He much lamented the death of the Count of Artois, his brother, and said that the latter would have been most unwilling to abstain as did the Count of Poitiers from coming to see him, and that nothing would have prevented him from coming to see him on the galleys.

"He also complained to me about the Count of Anjou who was on his ship, that he never kept him company. One day he inquired what the Count of Anjou was doing, and was told that he was playing backgammon with my lord Gautier of Nemours. And, tottering through the weakness consequent on his sickness, he went there and took the dice and the boards and threw them into the sea; and was very wroth against his brother because he had so early begun to play with dice. But my lord Gautier was the best off, for he threw into his pouch all the money which was on the boards (and there was a good heap) and took it away."

St Louis had also a sister, very much like him in character and piety, the Blessed Isabella, born in March 1225, foundress with the king her brother, of the famous monastery of Longchamps, near Paris, where she died in odour of sanctity on February

23rd, 1270. In spite of the persuasions of the Pope himself, she had refused the most brilliant marriages to devote herself entirely to works of prayer and charity. One day when she had made a cap with her own hands, St Louis, who loved his sister very much, asked her, with much gracious insistence, to let him have it to cover his head at night. But she refused him, saying that it was the first cap she had made and she owed it to God; then she secretly sent it to a poor sick woman of whom she had charge. The death of Isabella caused the king much grief, but he bore it like a Christian, full of resignation, faith and zeal. He wished to be present at the funeral of the pious princess, and himself stood at the door of the monastic enclosure, so that none should pass in but those who by virtue of an order of Clement IV. had the right to enter. He knelt and prayed fervently by his sister's body, and after the ceremony he addressed an exhortation to the nuns of Longchamps, to soften the sorrow they felt at the loss of their foundress and to promise them his protection. Isabella of France has been formally numbered, since the 16th century, amongst the Blessed, in accordance with a bull of Pope Leo X., dated January 11th, 1521.

CHAPTER IV

FRIEND AND MASTER—JEAN, SIRE DE JOINVILLE
ST LOUIS'S SURROUNDINGS

FRIENDSHIP, that feeling so natural and so sweet to man, is not more excluded by saintliness than are family affections. Amongst the many examples which prove this we must not neglect that of St Louis, whose exalted rank made it more difficult for him to taste that enjoyment. He did, however, enjoy it, and his affection for the young seneschal of Champagne, which was returned, is one of the most touching features of his history, from which Jean de Joinville is inseparable in the threefold character of familiar friend, witness, and biographer.

Descended from a noble family, whose power was undeniably established from the first half of the eleventh century, which had attained in the following century the highest rank among the Barons of Champagne and which became famous during the Crusades, Jean de Joinville was born in the early months of 1225. "He opened his eyes," says M. Gaston Paris, "in that beautiful Castle of Joinville, at the foot of which was situated the town bearing the name of Joinville, and which commanded a distant view of the course of the Upper Marne and the whole country of Vallage." By the death of his elder brother and that of his father he became possessed, while yet a child, under his mother's guardianship, of the patrimonial fief and the high office of seneschal of the Counts of Champagne which had become hereditary in his family. His education was that of the young knights of his time, of those at least, whose childhood was surrounded with special care.

As M. Paris explains it, this education "consisted chiefly in the apprenticeship of the profession of arms—riding, tilting, exercise in the use of the lance and sword." The future seneschal of Champagne had, moreover, to prepare himself for the duties of his office, which consisted, besides military and important judicial functions, in the domestic supervision of the palace, in the courts held by the count, and in personal service on the prince at the courts which he attended, especially at meals, remarkable for the most punctilious etiquette, when the seneschal had the honour of carving before his master, a difficult art in which instruction was needed. Joinville had learnt it early, for in 1241, at the age of sixteen, he filled this office and carved before his lord, the King of Navarre, at the High Court of Saumur. His mother must have taught him the minute rules of polished courtesy, in which he still took pride in his old age as having vigilantly maintained. She no doubt associated him with her by degrees in the administration of his possession, so that in his turn he might be able to govern and find his way amidst the entanglement of rights and jurisdictions leading to incessant and often violent conflicts, which the development of the feudal system had gradually formed, penetrating into all relations of men. Every noble in the Middle Ages was a judge or at least a jury in constant requisition. The seneschal of Champagne, who generally presided at the solemn assemblies on "high days" at Troyes, needed thorough acquaintance with the customs by which the civil and criminal laws were governed; nor was this to be learnt from books; it was necessary to be present at the pleadings and learn from the discussions and counsels of experienced persons. Joinville had been gifted from birth with an open mind, keen observation, a good memory, a desire for instruction, and a sense of respect, combined with independence of character and mind. He was certainly a good listener, he had quickness of perception, a retentive memory and accuracy in its application. We can apply to him at these early years of his active life the words he said of St Louis's early days—"If he behaved well and wisely it was no wonder, for he acted on the counsels and guidance of his good mother who was with him, and those of the upright men who had remained about him since his father's death."

"But," remarks the same learned man, "in this practical and worldly education, where was the place for what we should call literary teaching?" And here is the answer suggested by the attentive study of the facts. "Joinville certainly learned to read and write; he wrote easily himself; we possess a few words written by him at the foot of five charters of 1293, 1294, 1298, 1312 and 1317, and the bold and free writing does not suggest a hand unaccustomed to write. For the neat copy of his works, Joinville no doubt used to employ professional transcribers, and that we can easily understand when we think of the need of regularity and clearness in those days. It is very probable also that he dictated and did not himself write his works; that was the custom of every layman, but he had no difficulty in writing or reading. Learning to read in the Middle Ages meant learning at least a little Latin, for from Latin books spelling was learnt until the eighteenth century; the future knight, however, seems to have gone further. In his memoirs he quotes a few fragments of Latin, not only beginnings of prayers or hymns which any one can remember, such as *Miserere mei Deus, Esto Domine, Te Deum laudamus, Ad te levavi animam meam, Veni Creator Spiritus*, but even a whole line of the CIV. Psalm; we cannot, however, see that he had read many religious or profane books in Latin. As for French books, which in his youth were numerous and increasing considerably during his long life, such an inquisitive mind as his, so fond of distractions, must assuredly have used these means of instructing and refreshing himself, but we find few traces of these readings in his writings. Still young when he arrived at the court of Thibaut, 'the songster,' he who did not disdain women's society, must have been initiated in the art of composing words and music of the love-songs and satires then so fashionable; but if he really attempted them, none of his attempts have come down to us."

Besides his slight knowledge of literature, Joinville added to his taste for learning and letters a decided taste for the fine arts, "which is manifest,"

THE MAN

says M. Paris, " in many instances in that accomplished representative of the high society of the thirteenth century." He superintended himself the illustration, which he considered as important as the text itself, of his work on the *Credo*, and took no less care of that of the manuscript of his memoirs. He ordered pictures to be painted for the Chapel of St Laurence, and stained glass for the Church of Blécourt. Many years afterwards, he remembered with pleasure the " beautiful vignettes in fine gold " which he had seen on Oriental jewels; he admired and described the magnificent *ex voto* that Queen Margaret sent by him to St Nicholas of Varangeville; he was passionately fond of music, and had retained a pleasing recollection of the " Three Minstrels " of Armenia he heard at Jaffa, and their " sweet and gracious strains." It is true that he had no less admiration for the " wonderful capers " they performed.

Joinville was brought up in a profound and salutary habit of faith and Christian practice, and he took pleasure in developing and explaining his religion by meditation and frequent conversations with learned ecclesiastics with whom he was brought into familiar intercourse, either through his position or the circumstances of his life. St Louis helped him not a little to strengthen his knowledge in this direction, and to deepen his zeal. Under this saintly influence, he made an act of apostleship, when staying at Acre in 1250 and 1251, by writing a somewhat eloquent commentary for the use of the laity on the *Credo*, with the assistance of symbols and prophecies. This work was illustrated with paintings, so that the effect might be increased and might profit even the illiterate. This idea is not without analogy to that of an illustrated catechism. " You can see hereafter the articles of our Faith, painted and written in words and pictures. . . . Brother Henri le Tyois, a great scholar, says that none can be saved who does not know his *Credo*, and in order to incite people to believe what is indispensable, I had this work done in Acre after the departure of the king's brothers, and before the king went to fortify the city of Cæsarea in Palestine." The faith and piety of the good seneschal, though sincere and firm, never rose as far as asceticism; a man of pure morals, he ever retained an extremely lay and masterful temper, not without certain prejudices, and an unconscious touch of worldly and feudal malignity towards devotees, scholars, monks, prelates, and the See of Rome. His ever-recurring temporal quarrels with the Abbey of St Urbain, near his castle, in which he often seems to have been in the wrong, maintained his natural and hereditary disposition, but did not prevent him from being spiritually an obedient son of the Church. "We must believe the Holy Church of Rome, and must obey the commands the Pope and the prelates of Holy Church lay down for us, and perform the penances which they enjoin." Except as regards his feudal rights, interests and claims, he was ready to show the most tender veneration to the priests and religious whom his somewhat stern criticism judged to be worthy of their sacred calling, and he willingly consented to submit all worldly greatness to acknow-

THE MAN

ledged holiness. Summing up the principal traits of Joinville's character, M. Gaston Paris says: " He was naturally frank and cheerful ; he possessed a quick, active and open mind, but somewhat limited in perception, not capable of complicated reasoning, and inaccessible to ideas of any great breadth ; he was upright, loyal, faithful to his private as well as his public duties ; always just in his intentions, although liable to be influenced by passion ; he was naturally independent, saying all that came into his mind ; he was argumentative, talkative, and even somewhat of a gossip ; he did not lack self-confidence ; he was fond of advising others, but did not himself reject advice ; in a word, he was thoroughly good, and had a tender, charitable heart, made for friendship and family affection."

The undying bond which united St Louis and Joinville began during the Crusade. The seneschal had been induced to join this distant and perilous expedition by the purest Christian zeal. During their stay in Cyprus, the king, learning that Joinville had already nearly exhausted the resources he had procured before his departure, took him into his service for a year for a sum of two thousand livres. The young baron of Champagne was one of the first to land before Damietta, in the face of the enemy, and took an active part in the engagements which followed, showing great valour on the day of the battle of Mansourah. His heroic defence of a bridge thrown over a streamlet from the Nile, probably saved the king and his battalion from being surrounded by the enemy.

"We came to a small bridge which was over the stream and I said to the Constable that we should stay to guard it; for if we left it they would throw themselves on the king by its means, and our people might be overwhelmed if they were assailed on both sides. And thus we did. . . .

"Straight to us, who were keeping the little bridge, came Count Peter of Bretagne, who was coming straight from Mansourah and was wounded by a swordcut on the face, so that the blood flowed into his mouth. He was on a low, well-built horse; he had thrown the reins on his saddle-bow, which he was holding with both hands for fear that his men who were behind and pressing on him should make the horse go out of a walk. He seemed to care little about them, for when he spat the blood from his mouth he often said: 'Ha! by God's head, have you ever seen such fools?' Behind his battalion came the Count of Soissons and my lord Peter of Neuville, whom they call Caier, who had fighting enough for that day.

"When they had passed and the Turks saw that we were holding the bridge they let them be, and also when they saw that our faces were turned towards them. I came to the Count of Soissons, whose first cousin I had married, and said to him: 'Sir, I think you would do well if you remained to guard this little bridge, for if we leave it these Turks whom you see here in front of you will rush over it and thus the King will be assailed in the rear and in front.' He asked me whether I would stay also if he stayed, and I answered 'Yes, very willingly.'

THE MAN

When the Constable heard that he bade me not leave until he came back, and that he would go and seek help for us.

"We were covered with the Turkish darts. Now, it happened that I found a vest stuffed with flock on a Saracen; I turned the side which had been cut towards me, and made a shield of the vest which was of great use to me, for I was only wounded in five places by their darts while my horse was hit in fifteen places. Now it happened also that one of my men of Joinville brought me a banner bearing my arms and an iron lance, and every time we saw that they were pressing on the sergeants we ran upon them and they fled.

"The good Count of Soissons at this point joked with me and said: 'Seneschal, let these rascals howl, for by the head-piece of God (his usual oath), we shall talk of this again, you and I, in the ladies' withdrawing-rooms.

"In the evening at sunset the Constable brought us the cross-bowmen of the king, and they ranged themselves in front of us; and when the Saracens saw them draw the bows they fled and left us. And then the Constable said to me: 'Seneschal, this is well; now go to the King and do not leave him until he has dismounted at his tent.' As soon as I came to the king my lord John of Valery came to him and said, 'Sire, my lord of Chatillon begs you to give him the rear-guard.' This the king did willingly and then went his way. While we were going I made him take off his helm and lent him my steel cap so that he might have some air."

Joinville had his full share of the suffering and perils which assailed the king and those of the barons who survived the disastrous retreat of the Christian army, and the captivity which followed it. After the treaty with the enemy was concluded, Joinville crossed from Damietta to Acre on the same boat as the king and, so to say, by his side. "Then," says M. Paris, "the sympathy which had no doubt already in France drawn together these two men, one of whom, inferior in age and virtues was yet so well able to understand and love the other; an sympathy which must have been strengthened during the long stay in Cyprus and the trials of the Egyptian campaign was changed into a real friendship which lasted in the heart of the survivor until the end of his long life." Joinville seems to have been destined to excite the affection of St Louis by the resemblances and differences of their characters, by the qualities and the defects of the young seneschal, the first of which were really attractive to the heart of the pious king, while the latter gave him opportunities, according to the doctrinal bent of his mind, to correct them with a smile. That which above all appealed to the perfectly upright and loyal soul of St Louis was the bold sincerity of that frank and open nature in which a slight touch of banter and mischief, never overstepping the limits of a respect which at first rose to veneration, was not misplaced. Joinville's sallies shed bright rays of innocent merriment on the serious mind and austere habits of his royal friend.

Their mutual attachment grew more and more by

their constant and familiar relations during their sojourn of four years in Syria. Not only did the king renew the salary bestowed at Cyprus, but by an Act dated at Jaffa in April 1253, he granted to the seneschal of Champagne, in consideration of his services, an annual and hereditary stipend of two hundred livres; in virtue of which Joinville became his immediate vassal and, as the term was, his liegeman. Joinville came back to France on the royal vessel, and, in consequence of an accident which might have had fatal results, St Louis entrusted to him the supervision of the extinction of the fires.

"Before we reached land another adventure befell us at sea, which was this, that one of the queen's maids, after helping the queen to bed, did not take care, and threw the wrapper round her head near the iron stove on which the queen's candle was burning; and when she had gone to bed in the chamber below the queen's chamber, where the women slept, the candle burnt down till the stuff caught fire, and from the stuff it caught the cloths with which the queen's dresses were covered.

"When the queen awoke she saw that the chamber was all on fire, and jumped out of bed naked, took the stuff and threw it all aflame into the sea, and took the cloths and extinguished them. Those who were in the boat cried out in low voices 'Fire! Fire!' I raised my head and saw that the stuff was still burning brightly on the sea which was very calm. I put on my tunic as quickly as I could, and went to sit with the sailors.

"While I sat there, my squire, who slept in front

of me, came to me and told me that the king was awake, and that he had asked where I was. And I had told him that you were in the chambers, and the king said, 'You lie.' While we were speaking there, Master Geoffrey, the queen's clerk, came up and said to me, 'Be not afraid, for thus it chanced.' And I said to him, 'Master Geoffrey, go and tell the queen that the king is awake, and she must go and calm him.'

"The next day the Constable of France and my lord Peter the chamberlain, and my lord Gervais the steward, said to the king, 'What happened last night? we heard fire mentioned.' And I said not a word. And then the king said, 'It might well happen by misfortune that the seneschal is more discreet than I am, and I will tell you,' said the king, 'how nearly we were all burnt last night.'

"And he told them how it was, and said to me: 'Seneschal, I order you in future not to go to bed until you have put out all the lights here, except the great fire which is in the lower part of the ship. And know that I will not go to bed until you come back to me.' And thus did I all the while we were at sea, and when I came back, then the king would go to bed."

On his return to France, Joinville resumed the administration of his lands and the exercise of his high duties at the court of the Count of Champagne. But these occupations, says M. Paris, did not prevent him from often coming to Paris. His position obliged him to accompany his lord there on certain solemn occasions; thus he fulfilled his duties at the

THE MAN

nuptials of Prince Philip, the king's eldest son, in 1262, and at the festivities when this prince was knighted at Pentecost, 1267. On both these occasions he had a slight disappointment. The seneschal had a right to the dishes which had been used at the banquets of the Count of Champagne, nor was this a perquisite to be disdained, for the dishes were generally of silver and gold. After these two banquets he claimed the vessels which had adorned the table of his lord, but was told that they belonged to the King of France, and that the Count of Champagne had no right to them.

But Joinville did not come to Paris only as a follower of the Count of Champagne; he had become, as we have seen, the king's man, and had been attached by St Louis to his council; he took part both in the government of the kingdom and in the administration of justice. He was among those who judged what were then known as the "*plaids de la porte*," which are now called the Court of Requests; they also were about the king when, in his apartments, in the palace gardens or under the oak of Vincennes, about which we should know nothing were it not for the seneschal's charming description, he gave final decision in the lawsuits which had been reserved for his judgment or in which the parties appealed. Joinville himself mentions several occasions on which he was present at the king's council.

"The duties he had to perform at the king's council and the need of attending to his personal affairs, were not the only motives which drew Joinville so often to Paris, Corbeille, Poissy, Fontainebleau, Rheims or Orleans. The king was always pleased to see him and gave him quite exceptional proofs of his affection. During these visits of the seneschal, Louis would question him concerning what he thought of God, his horror of sin, or the pious works on which he engaged; encouraging him constantly to go forward in the ways of perfection, recommending him to honour the Saints, our mediators with God, or teaching him the sure means of being honoured in this world and saved in the next."

Thus did the pious king carry on the affectionate education of his young friend which he had begun during the Crusade, and in which his solicitude would sometimes stoop to give him advice pleasantly blended on morals or hygiene. " He asked me, when I was in Cyprus, why I did not mix water with my wine; I replied that it was by order of the doctors who said that I had a large head and a cold stomach and could not get drunk. He told me that they were deceiving me, for if I had not learnt to dilute wine in my youth and did not wish to do so in my old age, I should suffer from gout and stomach complaints so that I should never have good health; while, if I drank neat wine in my old age, I should be drunk every night and that was too ugly a thing for a valiant man."

Joinville fully appreciated the honour and advantage of being sermonised in this pleasant manner by such a king as St Louis. He was not, however, sorry to preach a little in his turn, as we have before seen; and his royal friend did not hesitate, in such a case, with perfect frankness to acknowledge the truth of his remarks and to profit by his advice. The good seneschal relates with visible pleasure an example of this.

"The king landed at the Castle of Hyères, with the queen and his children. While the king was staying at Hyères to procure horses to come to France, the Abbot of Cluny, who afterwards became bishop of Olive, made him a present of two palfreys which would to-day be well worth five hundred livres, one for himself and the other for the queen. When he had given him this present he said to the king: 'Sire, I will come to-morrow to speak to you about my own affairs.' On the following day the abbot came back; the king listened to him very attentively and at great length. When the abbot had gone I came to the king and said: 'I beg leave to ask whether you listened more kindly to the Abbot of Cluny because he gave you the two palfreys yesterday?'

"The king thought for a long time and then said, 'Yes, truly.' 'Sire,' said I, 'do you know why I ask you this?' 'Why?' said he. 'Sire,' said I, 'it is because I would advise and counsel you when you return to France, that you forbid all your sworn counsellors to accept anything from those who have business with you, for you may be sure that if they get anything, they will listen more willingly, and more attentively to those who give them presents, as you have done with the Abbot of Cluny.' Then the king called all his councillors and told them what I had said, and they told him that I had given him good advice."

Joinville's familiarity, though somewhat bold, would never have trespassed beyond certain limits; it lessened but never suppressed the distance between the seneschal of Champagne and the king of France. St Louis would not have permitted it. His natural and acquired kindness was kept in check by a great sense of dignity, prudence and kingly tact. St Louis, remarks M. Gaston Paris, was excessively reserved on certain subjects. Joinville was surprised and complained that during the five years they lived side by side, the king never mentioned the queen or the children she had borne him, and he adds with his habitual candour, "it seems to me that it was not a good habit to be a stranger towards his wife and children. Rather towards his confidential friends—even the dearest—St Louis became a 'stranger' regarding those subjects which he considered too intimate to be freely discussed."

The seneschal, in his turn, did not fear to maintain his independence of opinion and conduct. He gave a clear proof of this as regards the Crusade in Tunis. St Louis very much wished to take him with him. "It happened that the king summoned all his barons to Paris during one Lent. I excused myself from going on the plea that I then had a quartan fever and begged him to forgive my absence, and he sent word that he absolutely insisted on my going, for he had good doctors there who knew well how to cure quartan fever. . . .

"I was much pressed by the king of France and the king of Navarre to take the Cross; to which I replied that, while I was serving God and the king

THE MAN

over-seas, and since I had returned, the soldiers of the king of France and the king of Navarre had destroyed my property and impoverished my people, so that there would never be a day in which we should be in greater need. And I told them that if I wished to please God, I would remain here to help and defend my people; for if I put my body in peril by the pilgrimage of the Crusade, when I clearly saw that it would be to the detriment of my people, I should incur the wrath of God who gave His Body to save His people. . . ."

" They sinned greatly who advised him to make that journey when his body was so weak, for he could not bear to drive in a coach nor to ride on horseback. His weakness was so great that he allowed me to carry him in my arms from the count of Auxerre's house, where I took leave of him, to the Cordeliers."

We can see Joinville at that last interview, carrying as gently as possible in his good strong arms (he was nearly six feet) the emaciated body of his holy friend who did not return alive from Tunis, and whom he survived for nearly half a century. In 1282 he was one of the witnesses heard during the process for the canonisation, and he vigorously expressed the conviction "that he had never seen a man more adorned with the greatest perfection of all that can be seen in man." Then no doubt he must have remembered the amusing outburst which escaped him one day in Syria when he had undertaken to introduce to the king a band of Armenian pilgrims.

"From march to march we came to the sands of Acre, where the king and the army encamped. There a large band of people from Armenia came to me; they were going on a pilgrimage to Jerusalem, and were paying much tribute to the Saracens who guided them. They begged me, through an interpreter who knew their language and ours, to show them the 'saintly king.'

"I went to the king who was sitting in a tent, leaning against the tent-pole, and he was sitting on the sand, without carpet or anything else under him. I said to him: 'Sire, there is a great crowd of people from Armenia outside, going to Jerusalem, and they beg, Sire, that I will show them the saintly king; but I do not yet wish to kiss your bones.' And he laughed aloud and told me to go and fetch them; and so I did."

In 1297 he had the joy of seeing the Church authentically adjudge the aureole already attributed by public opinion to his royal friend during his life. With his enthusiastic veneration and his somewhat superficial theology, he considered that this aureole deserved an additional ray. "It seems to me," said he, "that they did not do enough for him when they did not put him in the ranks of the martyrs for the great sufferings he endured on the Pilgrimage of the Cross, during six years which I passed in his company, and because, above all, he imitated Our Lord on the cross. For if God died on the cross, so did he, for he was crucified when he died at Tunis." As M. Gaston Paris reminds us, "he was anxious to assist at the solemn exhumation of the body, which took place on the 25th August 1298. Brother John of Samois, who preached the sermon, mentioned the instance of loyalty towards the Saracens which Joinville had related. 'And do not think that I am telling you a lie,' added he, 'for I see here a man who gave me his oath that it is true'; and he indicated the seneschal upon whom all eyes were turned, and who must have experienced deep emotion."

The image of St Louis and of their friendship, stronger than death, presented itself to his mind and heart one night in an expressive manner, of which he has left us a touching account.

"I wish further to speak, hereafter, of our saintly king, some things which will be to his honour and which I saw of him in sleep; that is to say, it seemed to me in my dream that I saw him before my chapel at Joinville, and he was, it seemed to me, wonderfully joyful and glad of heart; and I was very glad myself because he was in my castle, and I said to him: 'Sire, when you leave this place I will lodge you in a house of mine situate in my village called Chevillon.' And he replied laughingly and said, 'Sire de Joinville, on the faith I owe you, I do not wish to set out so soon.'

"When I awoke I began to think, and it seemed to me that it pleased God and him that I should lodge him in my chapel, and so I did; for I set up an altar to God's and his honour, where they will sing for ever to his honour, and it is endowed with a perpetual dole for this purpose. And I narrated those things to my lord King Louis, who has inherited his name; and it seems to me that it would be pleasing to God and our saintly King Louis, if he procured some relics of the real sacred body and sent them to the said chapel of St Laurence at Joinville, that those who come to his altar may feel greater devotion."

This pious desire does not appear to have been fulfilled. But we cannot doubt that, in the absence of relics, the remembrance of his saintly friend, of their familiar intercourse, their conversations so fertile in edifying remarks, were most dear to Joinville, and the consolation of a long and green old age, universally respected, but not exempt from either trouble or sorrow, nor even from strife and lawsuits. The decline of the feudal aristocracy before the growing and daily more absolute power of the Capetian monarchy, led by its counsellors the imperial legislators, as also by the very exercise of its authority and the national temperament, far beyond the limits respected and the balance maintained by St Louis, the unscrupulous policy and crimes of Philip the Fair, were causes for painful regret and sources of bitterness, for the old seneschal, who daily became more and more the survivor of a vanished age, as may be seen by certain notable indications. He sought comfort in the frequent reminiscences of the days of his youth and of the men of an earlier time, chief among which always arose the sublime form of the king and saint who had loved him, and by whose side he had himself lived with honour.

He had begun somewhat early the agreeable custom of relating his reminiscences, sufferings

THE MAN

and adventures beyond seas, to those around him, and also to those whom he knew in high society and in conversation in ladies' withdrawing-rooms. Towards the year 1272, when he was about fifty, he even seems to have dictated to one of the clerks attached to his offices at Joinville, an account in the form of personal memoirs which he kept about him. Thirty years later, the heiress of his lords, Jeanne of Champagne and of Navarre, queen of France through her marriage with Philip the Fair, who had no doubt often heard and enjoyed the tales of the seneschal, in which St Louis naturally occupied a prominent position, asked him to compose for her a special book " of the saintly words and good actions " of the august prince, the pride of the house of France, whom he had known so intimately. Joinville set to work, taking as the basis of his labours the memoirs already prepared under his dictation, and he thus completed at the age of eighty that masterpiece of simple and striking narrative which, in spite of the general incoherence of construction and the inexperience of the author in the art of classifying his reminiscences and his thoughts, and of expressing them with elegance, exception also being made for some defects of information and of memory and some prejudice or worldly and feudal party-feeling, certainly deserves the immortality which, after long neglect, it has henceforth acquired, not only as one of the best sources of our history, but as one of the most precious monuments of our language and our literature.

Queen Jeanne was unable to enjoy it. She died

just when it was finished on the 2nd April 1305. Joinville transferred the homage and dedication of it to Prince Louis, Jeanne's son, and consequently King of Navarre and Count of Champagne, whom he lived to see mount the throne of France through the death of Philip the Fair (November 29, 1314), and descend from it, two years later, by his own death (June 5, 1316). It was only during the reign of Philip the Tall, fourth successor of St Louis, that according to M. Gaston Paris' expression, age at last triumphed over the indomitable vigour of body and soul of the old seneschal. He died, on the 24th December 1317, in his ninety-third year.

Joinville occupies, in the eyes of posterity, by the originality of his character and talent, a special position in the environment of St Louis; but, according to the few indications which have reached us, the group to which he belonged, or at any rate a good many of its members, would have been worthy, not only of the consideration, but of the pious respect of history. In this matter the youth of St Louis, under the care of Blanche of Castile, had been favoured by heaven. "The royal household, says M. Berger, was full of good counsellors, of those trustworthy knights and clerks who had been educated at the school of Philip Augustus; the young king loved to seek their advice. He had been struck by this precept which had been taught him: 'A bad emperor or a bad king is less to be feared than bad counsellors, because it is easier for many men to influence one, than for one to influence many.' Therefore the religious and wise prince took special care, after his majority, to choose his counsel and his household, which in many cases, owing to the customs of the Middle Ages, were practically the same. We find the traces of this judicious care in the following clause of the instructions addressed to his son Philip. 'Dear son, take care that your company be composed of upright men, whether religious or secular, and flee the society of the wicked, and hold good converse willingly with the good.'"

Among the knights of high or medium nobility honoured with the confidence and friendship of St Louis, it is good to mention at least these few names:—Simon of Nesle, one of the two regents of the kingdom during the Crusade of Tunis; John, Count of Soissons; Imbert of Beaujeu, Constable of France, and Gilles le Brun, who became Constable after him; Jean de Beaumont; Peter, called the chamberlain because he filled that position in the king's household, "the man," says Joinville, "whom he, St Louis, trusted most in the world, who, dying in Africa, obtained the honour of being buried at St Denis at his master's feet, where he had during his life-time slept for so long"; another chamberlain named Peter, called Peter of Laon, who also served St Louis during many years, and, says the confessor of Queen Margaret, "slept at his feet, took off his shoes and helped him to bed, as the squires of noble lords are accustomed to do"; Philip the Bold made him guardian of his children, and he was one of the witnesses who were heard in the process for the canonisation of the late king; he then declared especially that he had been cured at the

Palace of the Louvre of a violent pain in the arm, by applying to it the hair of St Louis which he had kept in memory of his dear master; the steward Gervais, another Gervais surnamed d'Escraine, the king's head barber; Geoffrey of Villette, Peter of Fontaines, Matthew of Marly, Philip of Nanteuil, Geoffrey of Sargines, and lastly Gautier or Gaucher Châtillon.

Geoffrey of Sargines was one of this group of "good knights" whom Joinville shows us as especially surrounding and guarding St Louis during the crusade. " I went, fully armed, to speak to the king, and found him fully armed, seated on a chair, and with him the brave men, fully armed, who were with the king, because there were eight with him, all good knights, who had had prizes for feats of arms at home and abroad, and such knights were generally called good knights." The king himself, when relating his disastrous retreat, told the seneschal in what manner Geoffrey of Sargines had performed his high office in these terms: "And the king told me that he was mounted on a small barb covered with a silken cloth; and he said that behind him there remained of all the knights and men-at-arms only my lord Geoffrey of Sargines, and he brought the king as far as the village where the king was captured; and the king told me that my lord Geoffrey of Sargines defended him from the Saracens in the same way as a good servant defends his lord's cup from the flies, for each time that the Saracens approached him, he took his lance, which he had placed between him and his saddle-bow, and putting it under his arm began to run after them again and drove them away from the king."

Gaucher of Châtillon, the leader of the rear-guard in this same retreat, met the heroic death of Robert the Strong at Brissarthe and of Roland at Roncevaux. It is, when rendered by the truthful and vivid brush of Joinville, a scene from a Christian Iliad:—

"I will not forget some things which happened in Egypt while we were there. First of all I will tell you about my lord Gaucher de Châtillon, about whom a knight, whose name was my lord John of Monson, told me how he saw my lord of Châtillon in a road of the village where the king was taken; and this road passed straight through the village, so that the fields could be seen both on one side and on the other. In this road was my lord Gaucher of Châtillon, with his drawn sword in his hand.

"When he saw that the Turks were coming along the road he ran upon them, sword in hand, and drove them out of the village; and the Turks flying before him, they who could shoot as well from behind as in front all covered him with darts. When he had hunted them from the village, he got rid of the darts he had on him, and put on his coat of mail again, then rose in his stirrups and stretched out his arms with the sword, crying: 'Châtillon, knight, where are my men-at-arms?' When he turned round and saw that the Turks had entered by the other end, he began again to run upon them sword in hand, and pursued them; and thus he did three times in the manner above described.

"When the admiral of the galleys had brought me to those who were taken on land, I enquired of those who were about him; but I could not find anyone to tell me how he was taken, except that my lord Jean Fouinon, the good knight, told me that when he was taken as a prisoner to Mansourah, he found a Turk who was mounted on my lord Gaucher of Châtillon's horse, and the horse's crupper was all bloody. And he asked what he had done to the owner of the horse; and the Turk replied that he had cut his throat while he was on the horse, as was plain by the crupper which was covered with blood."

The prelates and clerks formed part with the barons and knights of the group of counsellors and friends of St Louis, and the pious king did not, of course, show to them less confidence than to the latter. Among those who obtained it and lived, at least from time to time, in intimacy with the monarch are two who became popes: Guy Foucaud under the name of Clement IV., and later, Simon of Brion under the name of Martin IV. The bishops of Paris were, by force of circumstances, habitual members of the council, or at any rate visitors and frequent guests of the royal palace. We find traces of the intercourse and familiar conversations of St Louis with William of Auvergne, the eminent theologian and philosopher who filled the episcopal see from 1228 to 1248. His successors, Gautier of Chateau-Thierry, Renaud of Corbeil, Stephen Tempier seem also to have enjoyed the favour of their august diocesan, who placed the last-named prelate among his testamentary executors. An ecclesiastic of secondary rank, however, the famous founder of the College of Sorbonne, Robert of Sorbon, a man of humble birth, but of great knowledge and exalted virtue, occupied in the estimation and affections of St Louis a similar position to that of the sire de Joinville. One of his delights was to have them both by him together, and to hear them hold, not without some vivacity, the little disputes in which they were often engaged by the differences in their positions and tempers. But one day they both drew a reproof upon themselves. "Owing to the great renown which he had as a man-at-arms, the king made Maitre Robert of Sorbon dine at his table. One day it happened that he was seated by me and we were talking together in a low voice. The king reproved us and said, 'Speak louder, for your companions think that you may be speaking against them. If while you dine you speak of things which may be agreeable, speak out—if not, be silent.'" Those of his biographers who knew him best noted the pleasure he showed in admitting to his table the persons, clerks or laymen whose virtues and merits he had heard extolled, who were within his reach. Two of these very biographers, without counting Joinville, enjoyed the honour of his edifying friendship — Geoffrey of Beaulieu his confessor and William of Chartres. The latter, said Tillemont, was clerk or almoner of St Louis in the year 1250, and kept him company in his captivity. St Louis afterwards gave him a very rich treasurership and then said laughingly to Geoffrey of Beaulieu, "Monsieur William will amuse himself with his benefice for five or six years and then will enter into religion." William, who was present, said he had no intention of becoming a religious and he had no wish to do so then. But at the end of five and a half years he accomplished St Louis's prophecy, of which he thought no more, and became a Franciscan.

Below the knights and clerks of the royal palace, the household of St Louis included, of course, more humble servants, to whom the word "domestics," used in its modern sense, would apply more properly. Yet there seems to have been among them several of good middle class condition, and in any case, we know some who gained great honour, by their fidelity and virtues, in the most intimate circle of the pious monarch. Such especially was Isembart, described in the list of witnesses heard for the canonisation, as " Isembart, the cook of the blessed King St Louis, a rich man of mature age, born in Paris, and fifty-five years old, or thereabout." He had shared his master's captivity, and had rendered him truly filial attentions during his illness. Such again was Gaugelme, one of his valets, whom he loved much, who, on his side, felt so deep an affection for the king, that when lying ill in the camp near Mansourah, and at the point of death, he said to William of Chartres, " I am expecting the visit of the saintly king, my lord, and I will not leave this world until I have seen and spoken with him, and then I shall not delay to die." It was so, William tells us. " For a few minutes after the king came to see him, and consoled him with pious words. Then, going away, he had not yet reached his tent, when he was informed that Gaugelme had just breathed his last.”

St Louis's servants, in spite of the veneration they must have felt for such a master, sometimes tried his heroic patience, as we shall see. Indeed, Ponce, one of his squires, tired him out one day. Of course we owe this anecdote to Joinville.

"The day the king left Hyères (when returning from the Crusade), he descended from the castle on foot, because the hill was too steep; and he went so far on foot that, because he could not have his palfrey, he had to mount mine. And when his palfrey came, he ran up, very much irritated against Ponce the squire; and when he had rated him well, I said, 'Sire,' you must excuse many things in your squire Ponce, for he served your grandfather, and your father and you."

"Seneschal," said he, "he did not serve us; we served him when we allowed him near us with the bad qualities which he has. For my grandfather King Philip told me that we should reward our people, one more, another less, according to their services; and he said, moreover, that none could be a good ruler if he did not know how to refuse boldly and harshly, as he knew how to give. And I teach you these things, said the king, because this age is so greedy of asking, that there are few who think of the salvation of their souls or their personal honour, if only they can get another's goods for themselves, by foul means or fair."

St Louis's most hasty actions became of themselves, as may be seen, occasions for sound teaching, hints, and useful advice. He did not neglect the spiritual interests and moral improvement of the people of his household. He laboured at this personally. "Often when he was in his chamber with his household, says the confessor of Queen Margaret, he said holy and wise words, and told beautiful stories for the edification of those who were about him. He vigilantly enquired into the behaviour of his servants, and if he has made us admire his mercy towards such acts as caused him personal injury, as for instance, those thefts of money committed against him, which he merely punished by obliging the delinquent to stay in the Holy Land; yet when justice, morals, or religious principles were in question, he exercised, without weakness in his household, his double authority as a king and father, by inflicting appropriate punishments. We may, perhaps, even think that if his heroic virtue made him lean towards indulgence, yet, by nature, he would rather have been stern. He was a tender-hearted saint, but his mind and will were strong.

CHAPTER V

THE CHRISTIAN—THE RELIGIOUS AND MORAL VIRTUES OF SAINT LOUIS

IF there is anyone to whom the faith received in baptism becomes the very foundation of moral life and character, St Louis was certainly that man. We know that he liked to be called Louis of Poissy, because he was baptized in that town. The steadfast foundation of all his thoughts, all his acts and feelings, was the conviction of the absolute truth of the Christian religion. We believe it to be the result of one of these strange and deceptive fancies with which sophistical incredulity has imbued even able minds, that M. Langlois has represented him as sometimes tormented by the contradictions which exist between common sense and faith. Not only are these assured contradictions a chimera, but the steadfast mind of St Louis, and the deeply religious environment in which he lived from his earliest childhood can have afforded little scope for the temptation of doubt. It was not so much from personal experience, as from his acquaintance with theology, asceticism and mysticism, that he was aware of the danger of this temptation, and pointed out its danger to Joinville:

"The saintly king, in what he said, endeavoured with all his might to establish my belief in the

Christian law which God has given us. He said that we ought to believe the articles of faith so firmly that neither death nor any bodily evil would dispose us to oppose it in words or actions, and he said that the enemy is so subtle that when men are at the point of death he does all that he can to make them die in some doubt on matters of faith; for he sees that he cannot take from men the good works which they have done; and he also sees that they are lost to him if they die in the true faith.

"Wherefore we must be careful to keep and defend ourselves from this snare, in such manner as to say to the enemy when he sends any like temptation: 'Get thee gone,' let him say to the enemy, 'thou shalt not tempt me so as to shake my belief in all the articles of faith; even if thou shouldest cause all my limbs to be cut off, I will live and die in this faith.' Whoso acts thus conquers the enemy with the weapon and sword by which the enemy sought to slay him.

"He said that we must hold fast to faith and credence, even if we were only assured of it by hearsay. On this point he asked me what was my father's name. I told him that his name was Simon. Then he asked me how I knew this, and I told him that I was assured of it, and believed it firmly, on the witness of my mother. Then he said to me: 'Then you should firmly believe all the articles of faith, to which the apostles bear witness, as you hear chanted in the *Credo* every Sunday."[1]

---

[1] Joinville, as we have seen, was still an infant when his father died.

THE MAN

The faith of St Louis was therefore not a tormented faith, but thoughtful, reasonable, and, as we may say, armed at all points. It was deeply seated and solidly intellectual, as it appears from the stories he liked to tell Joinville. One in particular deserves to be recalled, as it contains a lesson which applies to those persons who are too fond of material forms of piety and miraculous manifestations. "The saintly king told me that many of the Albigenses came to the count of Montfont, who at that time kept the land of the Albigenses for the king, and told him that they came to see our Saviour's body, which became flesh and blood in the hands of the priests. And he said to them : ' Go and see it, you who do not believe. As for me, I firmly believe it just what Holy Church tells us of the Sacrament of the Altar. And do you know what I shall gain,' said the count, 'because I believe in this mortal life all that Holy Church teaches ? I shall have a crown in heaven above the angels who see him face to face ; and for this cause they must believe.' "

St Louis rightly considered that it was not fitting lightly to expose this faith, which he was justified in regarding as the great treasure of the Christian soul, to the assaults of armed incredulity; in this respect he made a wise distinction between the clergy and the laity, expressed by him in familiar conversation with a humorous vehemence, and it would, we think, be somewhat dense to take these pious sallies literally. M. Langlois's description of his mode of viewing the subject may, to a certain extent, be accepted : " He liked to hear those who defended the faith, not those who attacked it. He was no partisan of the disputes of Christians with Jewish rabbis, of which the doctors of the thirteenth century were so fond. ' He told me,' says Joinville, ' of a great dispute between the clergy and the Jews at the monastery of Cluni. A knight, who was a guest at the monastery, rose and asked the chief teacher among the Jews if he believed the Virgin Mary to be the Mother of God. The Jew replied that he did not believe it. Then you are a fool to have come, replied the knight, "since you do not believe in the Blessed Virgin, and do not love her in her own house;" and he struck down the Jew by a blow on the head. ' And I tell you,' said the king, ' that only a very good clerk ought to dispute with such people; when a layman hears the Christian law reviled, he ought only to defend it with the sword, with which he should pierce the speaker's body, just as far as it will go.' " [1]

The saintly king's delicacy of conscience on this subject is clearly shown with respect to the oath exacted from him by the Saracen emirs for the confirmation of the treaty for his release. On the advice of some miserable apostates, they wished to impose upon him the stipulation that, if he did not hold to the conditions made, he should be as much dishonoured as the Christian who denies God and

[1] " I ought to observe," writes M. de Wailly in a note to the story, " that so far from putting this theory in practice, St Louis converted many Jews by persuasion, and attached them to him by his benefits." The pious king, who does not formally approve the knight's act, seems, moreover, to state the hypothesis of an attack on the Christian faith.

His law, and who contemns God by spitting and trampling on the Cross. St Louis firmly rejected the stipulation, as much on account of expressions which were abhorrent to him, as because he could not accept the supposition of apostasy, although his steadfast intention to execute the treaty rendered it purely imaginary. The threats of the Saracens to cut off his head, the entreaties of all his counsellors, and especially of his brother Charles, and of the Patriarch of Jerusalem, who offered to take the sin, if there was one, on himself, could not shake his resolution, and the emirs were obliged to give up the stipulation. Moreover, the courage, which was the natural result of his steadfast faith, his absolute confidence in God, and entire trust in Providence, added to his native firmness under such circumstances, a power of stern inflexibility, which might be said to subdue the violent cruelty of gaolers, who were ready to become his executioners.

"The Soldan's counsellors," writes Joinville, "treated the king as they had already treated us, in order to see whether the king would promise to surrender any of the strongholds belonging to the Temple or the Hospital, or any of the barons' strongholds, and, as it was the will of God, the king answered after the same manner as we had answered. Then they threatened him, and said that if he would not do it, they would put him into *barnacles*.

"These are the most cruel torment which it is possible to endure. Two pieces of flexible wood are furnished, with teeth at one end, which fit into each other, and are bound together with strong leather straps. When they are to be used, the man is laid upon his side with his legs within the boards; a man then sits on the pieces of wood, whence it follows that there is scarcely six inches of bone which is not completely crushed. To make it as bad as possible, after three days, when the legs are swelled, the swelled legs are replaced in the *barnacles*, and are crushed over again. The king replied to these threats, that he was their prisoner, and they could do what they pleased with him. They saw plainly that they could not overcome his courage, and must be content with such conditions as his conscience allowed him to accept. This attitude surprised them so much, that they said to him: 'It might truly be said that we are your captives, not that you are ours.'"

The same faith which inspired his heroic resignation sustained as foundation of his love the fervour of a zeal so ardent, that it is difficult with our colder temperament not to consider it as somewhat excessive. But the steadfast vision of St Louis always remained beneath this holy exaggeration, or, as we should rather say, beneath the transcendent and superhuman virtue which we cannot fail to commemorate and admire; and the discernment, perspicacity, wisdom, and prudence, with which his strong and upright soul was endowed, are apparent. The contemporary writers of his life have remarked his delicate reserve, as well as the amiable facility of his speech: "*cautissimus erat, et gratiosissimus in loquendo.*" Notwithstanding his strong natural taste for edification and the apostolate, he was able to distinguish between the practices of supererogation, dear to his asceticism, and the ordinary duties of Christian conduct, and he did not always advise an exact imitation of his own austerities.

Thus, although he renounced for himself not merely luxury, but any elegance in dress, and would not, it is said, give way to the queen's wishes on this point, Joinville tells us that, on the occasion of a dispute with Robert of Sorbon, he proposed a more moderate rule to the princes and great lords of his court. "You ought," he said, "to be well and properly dressed, since your wives will like you the better for it, and your dependants will esteem you more highly. For," he wisely added, "men ought to wear such clothes and armour that the sober men of our day ought not to think them too fine, nor should the young men think them too mean." He did not like the songs and tales of minstrels, nor even secular music, and William of Chartres tells us that he tried to turn away his children and friends from such follies. Yet Joinville expressly says that his pious repugnance on this point had not the character, even in his court and presence, of an absolute prohibition. Thus—no doubt on days of ceremony—when the minstrels of rich men brought their viols after a meal, he waited until the minstrel had ended his song before hearing grace. Then he rose, and the priests stood up before him in order to say their grace. And the seneschal adds, as if to show how his asceticism was tempered by a fitting and judicious liberty, "When we were in privacy at his court he would seat himself at the foot of his bed, and when the preachers and friars who were there spoke of a book, to which he willingly listened, he would say, 'You need not read to me, for there is no book after eating so good as talk *ad libitum*, that is, that each man would say what he will.' When rich men who were strangers ate with him, he was very companionable."

However great was his zeal for the austerities of penance, and we shall see that it was extreme, yet he knew how to moderate it under wise advice, either on account of his weakness of health or of his duties as a king. Thus his confessor, by appealing to this double motive, made him renounce the use of the hair shirt, although he was strongly attached to this mortification. The pious king, while caring little for the respect of man, kept a discreet reserve save with his intimate friends respecting a certain number of frequent acts of austerity, of charity, of superhuman charity, fearing lest the very elevation of his rank might in the case of weak souls change edification into scandal. On this account he bridled his zeal by prudent observances. Queen Margaret's confessor gives us an example, also related by Geoffrey of Beaulieu:

"According to the custom of the Cistercian order, certain monks in each abbey of this order, some at one time, some at another, when the abbot and the convent are assembled in the cloister, have to wash the feet of the other monks, thus doing what is called the *mandè* every Saturday after vespers. The pious king often visited the abbey of Royaumont, belonging to this order. When he happened to be there on Saturday, he wished to be present at the *mandè*, and seated himself beside the abbot, and very devoutly watched what the monks were doing. One day it happened that, in seating himself beside the abbot, he said to him, 'It would be well for me to wash the monks' feet.' The abbot replied, 'You would do better to refrain from this.' The pious king asked why, and the abbot answered, 'People would talk about it.' 'What would they say?' asked the pious king. The abbot answered that some would speak well and others ill of this act, and the pious king abstained from doing it, since the abbot dissuaded him. He had with him that day several nobles of the kingdom who were not among his intimate friends."

Queen Margaret's confessor says "that the virtue of justice which awards to every man his right was very manifest in the blessed St Louis." It was in fact the dominant quality of his moral character, and this human virtue, confirmed and sanctified by grace, was the foundation of the king's greatness. A signal proof of his scrupulous loyalty was given in the execution of the treaty contracted with the Egyptian emirs after the Saracens themselves had grossly violated its conditions. There was a question of the payment of the 200,000 livres which he was to hand over to them before embarking.

"When the payment was made," says Joinville, "the king's counsellors who were to pay it over came to him and said that the Saracens would not surrender his brother, Alphonse of Poitiers, until they had the money set before them. Every one in the council was of opinion that the king ought not to give up the money until he had his brother back. The king answered that he would pay, as he had promised, and that as for the Saracens they would keep their promises, if they thought good to do so. Then Monseigneur Philip of Nemours told the king that they had defrauded the Saracens of 10,000 livres.

"The king was greatly vexed, and said that he wished the 10,000 livres to be paid, since he had promised to pay the 200,000 livres before leaving the river. Then I trod on Monseigneur Philip's foot and told the king not to believe him, as he spoke untruly, for the Saracens were the most accurate reckoners who ever lived. Monseigneur Philip said that I was right, and that he had only spoken in jest. And the king said that such a jest was ill-timed. 'And I command you,' said the king to Monseigneur Philip, 'on the faith which you owe to me as my servant, that if the 10,000 livres are not paid, you shall pay them without fail.'

"Many people had advised the king to repair to his ship, which was waiting for him on the sea coast, so as to be out of the Saracens' hands. The king paid heed to none of them, but said that he would not leave the river, according to his promise, until the 200,000 livres were paid. As soon as payment was made, the king, without any entreaty, told us that he was now absolved from his oath, and that we might depart and go to the ship, which was on the sea coast."

If the deep sense of justice which penetrated the soul of St Louis may have contributed to the natural severity of which there are traces in his character, he was, on the other hand, influenced by his faith and transcendent charity, no stranger to the benevolent humanity which in every case tempered the king's natural severity. Kindness, in addition to its peculiar attractiveness, is part of the debt which every man may be said to have contracted at his birth, both to God and to his neighbour. This quality was natural in the saintly king, and also singularly developed by his sanctity; manifesting itself in the gracious, yet always dignified affability of his manner and speech, and, save in some exceptional circumstances, in the moderation and gentleness which he used ever in his reproofs. "Grace was spread upon his lips," says Geoffrey of Beaulieu, borrowing the words of Scripture, "and, like a truly wise man, he knew how to make his words lovable. We cannot fail to see in this fair soul the union of justice and kindness, and it is this burning love, and this almost passionate desire for peace between men which procured for him, as one of his essential titles, the noble name of 'the pacific king.'"

No doubt the austere asceticism of St Louis was greatly in excess of the ordinary virtue of temperance, which aims at rendering the Christian master of himself, and, above all, of his carnal desires. It is, however, not amiss to note that if his ecclesiastical biographers have, to his great honour, acquainted us with the enforcement and special refinements of his penitence, ingenious in its repression of every sensual impulse, Joinville has handed down to us what may be termed the general and common rule of his public behaviour, more generally apparent in the satisfaction of the natural needs of human life. "He was so sober in diet that he never ordered any food beyond what was prepared by his cook; he ate what was put before him. He poured his wine into a glass goblet, adding water according to its strength, and he held the goblet in his hand while the wine was poured in by one standing behind the table."

We have already seen, and shall have further occasion to see, with what power, magnanimity and heroic patience St Louis maintained his self-command during the critical circumstances of his life; during the disaster in Egypt, for instance, and in his captivity. But he was equally self-possessed in common life, and it is to this quality in particular that I think we ought to ascribe the noble traits of endurance and patience collected by Queen Margaret's confessor in the depositions presented on the inquiry into his canonisation.

"On one occasion, when the blessed king was in Paris, he left his chamber in order to hear causes and attend to business. After a long audience he returned to his chamber, only accompanied by the knight who usually slept in it. When he got there, none of his chamberlains or other servants were in, although there were sixteen, including the chamberlains, valets-de-chambre and bed-makers, who ought to have been in the chamber. They were called through the palace and the garden and elsewhere, and no one could be found to wait upon him. The knight who was with him wished to serve him, but the blessed king would not suffer him to do so. When a chamberlain and the other valets came back and learned that the king had not found a living soul in his chamber, they were much distressed and afraid, so that they did not dare to come into his presence; but they began to bemoan themselves before Brother Peter, of the Order of the Trinity, who joined with the blessed king in saying his Hours, and was much in his confidence and familiarity. When the king saw them as he was going back to hear causes, he took his hand from under his robe and said, 'So you have come at last; I have no one to attend to my needs, although one alone, even the least among you, would suffice.' He did not say another word, and returned to his causes. And when he went back to his chamber after the causes were ended, his chamberlains and the others still did not dare to come before him. Brother Peter said that they would never dare to come unless he shewed his clemency and caused them to be summoned. And he caused them to be summoned, and he began to laugh and said gaily, 'Come, come, you are sad because you have done amiss. I forgive you; take care to do so no more in future.'

"Now, on this same day the blessed king, after his usual day-sleep, wished to go to the wood of Vincennes, which is distant a league from Paris. The chamberlain, whose office it was, forgot to put the overcoat of which the king made use at meals in the coffer in which it was generally kept, but he put it in another coffer of which he had the key, and did not go to Vincennes, but remained in Paris.[1] When, therefore, the blessed king was at Vincennes and wished to sup, he asked for this overcoat, but it was not to be found in the coffers of which the keys were brought. The chamberlains who were present wished to break open the coffer in which they supposed the overcoat to be, but the blessed king would not allow it. He was therefore obliged to sup in his sleeved robe, and yet he showed no sign of anger and said not a word of the mistake, except that he said with a laugh to the knights who were eating supper with him, 'What do you think? Do I look well at table in my robe?' His household marvelled much at such patience, since after two such great faults had been committed in one day the blessed king was not more moved, nor even retained any grudge against them.

"Another time it happened when the blessed king was at Noyon that he was eating in his chamber, and some knights with him near the fire, for it was winter; and his chamberlains took their meal in an adjoining room, serving for his wardrobe. Now the blessed king, in his discourse with the knights, said this word: 'And this I maintain.' Now behold one of the chamberlains called John Bourguignet began to say by way of bravado against the king, 'You may say that you maintain it, but you are only a man like

[1] It was then the custom, as M. Langlois remarks, for men of rank to put on an overcoat like a blouse before eating, in order to keep their clothes unsoiled.

any other.' Monseigneur Peter of Laon, also a chamberlain, heard these words, which were indeed an outrage to so great a prince and their lord, and spoken without cause, since the said John had not been able to hear of what the king was speaking, for Monseigneur Peter who was more forward, had not heard it. He therefore drew John Bourguignet to him and said in a low voice, 'What did you say? Are you out of your senses to speak thus to the king?' And John replied, but so loud that it was impossible the king should not hear, 'Yes, yes, he is only a man, and just like any other.' As Monseigneur Peter testifies, the blessed king, who had heard the said John's words both the first and second time, looked at him in silence and told no more of his story, and did not in any way reprove him. Nor did Monseigneur Peter even perceive that, either in word or action, the king showed any resentment towards the said John Bourguignet.

"The blessed king was attacked by an illness three or four times a year, and he was sometimes much tormented by it. This illness was of such sort, when it attacked the king, that he became hard of hearing, and could not eat nor sleep, and he bemoaned himself with groans. The illness endured for about three days, more or less, and he was then unable even to be out of bed; and when he began to amend, his right leg, from the thigh to the ankle, became blood-red all over and swelled; and it remained with this redness and swelling from morning to night; then, little by little, this redness and swelling went away, so that on the third or fourth day the flesh of the leg became like that of the rest of the body, and the blessed king was then completely cured. Now several knights and either one or two chamberlains lay in his chamber, and usually an old servant lay there also; he was called John, had been watchman to King Philip, and it was his office to look after the fire both in summer and winter. It happened one evening when the blessed king was suffering from this illness, that he wished before getting into bed to look at the redness of his leg; and in order that he might do so, old John lighted a wax candle and held it above the king's leg, while he observed the redness and swelling which gave him so much pain. But the said John held the candle so clumsily that a drop of burning wax fell on the blessed king's leg, on the place where it was swelled and red. The king, who was sitting on his bed, was so much hurt that he threw himself back, saying, 'Ah, John!' And John said to him, 'Ah! I have hurt you.' And the blessed king answered, 'John, the last king would have sent you away for a slighter fault'; for the said John had told the king and Monseigneur Peter of Laon and others also of the royal chamber, how King Philip had once turned him away because he had put on the fire some logs which crackled as they burned. Yet, as Monseigneur Peter of Laon testified on oath, the saintly king was never at any time ill disposed towards John, whom he always kept in his service."

The religious and moral qualities of which we have just given an account, are in themselves, although carried by St Louis much beyond the average degree, the ordinary and common virtues of a good and loyal

Christian. In his own time they were so regarded, and he himself liked to sum them up as the qualities of an honest man. Joinville says that he expressed his feeling on the subject with that salt of human wit with which, among his intimates, he never failed to enliven from time to time the pious savour of his discourse. "When the king was in good spirits, he would say: 'Seneschal, tell me why an honest man is better than one who is devout.' Then arose a discussion between me and Master Robert. When we had disputed long, the king delivered his sentence, and spoke thus: 'Master Robert, I would rather be called an honest man, if such I am, and I leave all the rest to you; for this name of honest man (*prud'homme*), is such a great and good thing, that it fills the mouth even to speak it.'"

We must not, however, misunderstand St Louis's opinion, of which it may be taken as certain that the good seneschal, in accordance with his own inclination, accentuated, rather than attenuated, the exact expression. It would be a wrong interpretation, under the influence of the prejudices of our epoch, to say with M. Langlois that there never was a saint so much of a layman as this one. In the first place, St Louis did not apply the term *prud'homme* to laymen only, since Joinville himself says, as we have seen, that it was precisely in his quality of *prud'homme* that Robert of Sorbon obtained his friendship and intimacy with the saintly king. And, again, since it is now time to show him as he will appear in the ensuing pages, we shall see that St Louis added to the virtues of a perfect layman and perfect knight, not merely the piety of a perfectly devout man in the best sense of the word, but even perhaps to an exaggerated degree, the distinctive qualities and tastes of a priest and monk. "His mode of living and his actions," William of Chartres justly says, "were not only those of a king, but of a regular," that is, of a religious. The fact, therefore, is established that St Louis pleased both the sire de Joinville and Master Robert, in being the most *prud'homme* among the devout, and the most devout among *prud'hommes*.

CHAPTER VI

THE CLERK—THE INTELLECTUAL QUALITIES AND HABITS OF ST LOUIS

UNLIKE the sire de Joinville, whose literary education was merely elementary, St Louis had received in his youth a very careful culture, which he maintained and developed throughout his life. He knew Latin so well, that he was able to translate works written in that tongue with the book open before him, as he sometimes did when with his intimates. It is scarcely necessary to say that these works were of a religious and ecclesiastical character. The pious king's taste would not have inclined him to any other literature, and he had at the same time been guided to sacred writings by his education, which, in its advanced stage, was at that time necessarily the same as that given to the clergy. There is no doubt that St Louis had, among his other merits, the intellectual qualities and habits of the intelligent and studious clerks of his day.

The strict teacher who conducted his Latin studies, probably a Dominican or Franciscan religious, had doubtless given a colour to his lessons in grammar, and these were in any case supplemented by theology and philosophy. This must have been still more the case with the other teachers, who were directly or indirectly summoned in their turn to form and nourish his mind. M. Lecoy de la Marche writes that: "Elinand, a monk of the abbey of Froidmont, composed a treatise on the duties of princes which was probably used for his instruction, and in which the practice of learning is expressly recommended as indispensable. An unlearned king, he said, is only a crowned ass. Other religious, preaching or minor friars, and William of Auvergne, the great bishop of Paris, also contributed, as we cannot doubt, to the culture of this young intelligence, which spontaneously opened to receive all knowledge that was noble and salutary." As it appears from an anecdote told by him to Joinville, the young king had carefully retained in his mind the recollection of his conversations with the wise prelate; these appear to have had sometimes the character of a familiar teaching of theology, illustrated by examples.

The zealous faith of St Louis and his naturally doctrinal turn of mind, must have maintained that taste for religious knowledge which had been developed by his education. His saintly eagerness to hear sermons must doubtless be ascribed to his love of this knowledge, as well as to his fervent piety. "He loved much to hear the Word of God," Tillemont writes, "referring the information he received to the original texts. On Sundays and holidays, often even on working days, when he met with religious and others capable of giving instruction, he made them preach and listened to them with great care and devotion. When he was on a journey and in the neighbourhood of some monastery, he would, if not pressed for time, turn aside to go there, and would cause one of the house to preach. He listened to sermons seated on the ground or on a mat, however cold it might be. In the same posture he heard the instructions given to monks in their chapters, and yet desired them to keep their usual seats. This was particularly noticed once at Châlis, where he sat down on two paving-stones. At Royaumont he often sat on the mat which was placed beside a pier. He would sometimes go a quarter of a league out of his way on foot in order to hear a sermon, and return in the same way. He was careful himself to see that silence was kept. When sermons pleased him he could retain them in his memory and repeat them with much grace. On his return from Cyprus, sermons were preached on board his vessel three times a week."

This taste for sacred knowledge and clerical instruction is still more exactly shown in the facts reported as follows by Queen Margaret's confessor. "A doctor in theology was explaining the psalter at the abbey of Royaumont. Sometimes when the king was at this abbey, and he heard the bell which called the monks to go into the schools, he himself would come to the school and seat himself among the monks at the feet of the master who gave the lesson, as if he were himself a monk; he listened diligently; and this the pious king did repeatedly. And sometimes the pious king went into the schools of the preaching friars of Compiègne and seated himself on the pavement before the pulpit from which the master read, and listened diligently; the friars themselves sat on the high seats in use in the schools, and when they wished to come down from their seats and sit on the ground, the pious king would not allow it. It sometimes happened also that when he was in the refectory of the preaching friars of Compiègne, he would go up to the desk from which the Bible was read during meals, according to the friars' custom, and the pious king would stay for a long while beside the friar who was reading, and he listened with pleasure."

He satisfied the same noble instinct by a remarkable assiduity in personal study. "The blessed St Louis," the same author writes, " aware that time should not be spent on trifling matters, nor on curious and profane questions, but in more worthy and weighty occupations, applied himself to the reading of the Holy Scripture. He had a Bible with notes, and the original writings of St Augustine and of other saints. He often read or caused them to be read to him in the interval between his dinner and his mid-day sleep, at least when he took this sleep, which was seldom, and when compelled to take it he did not tarry in sleep. And he often resumed the reading after his sleep until vespers, when he was not encumbered with important affairs. At such times also he would willingly call in some religious or other worthy people, with whom he spoke of God, of his saints and their acts, and again of the narratives in Holy Scripture and of the lives of the Fathers. And moreover every day, when complines had been said in the chapel by his chaplains, he returned to his chamber; there a candle of a certain length was lighted, three feet or thereabouts, and so long as it lasted he read the Bible or some holy book; and when the candle was nearly burnt out, one of his chaplains was called, with whom the king said complines in private."

It is characteristic of St Louis's intellectual tastes, and it does honour to his noble mind, that he was not content to have books for his personal use; he resolved to form a library which should serve not only for his own studies, but for those of others. The religious emulation which, according to Geoffrey of Beaulieu, led to this resolution, does not diminish its merit. "The king," he tells us, "when he was beyond seas, heard it said of a great Saracen soldan that he had made diligent search for all sorts of works which might be necessary for the philosophers of his religion, and these were copied at his expense and kept in his palace, so that they might be used whenever it was needful. Judging from this that the sons of darkness are really more prudent than the sons of light, and more ardent zealots of error than the others are of Christian truth, the pious king determined that when he returned to France he would have copied at his expense all the useful and authentic books relating to Holy Scripture which could be found in the different abbeys, so that he himself, and the clerks and the religious with whom he was intimate, might study them for their own advantage and that of their neighbour. On his return he carried out this plan, and in order to do so he arranged a safe and convenient place, namely, the treasure-chamber to his chapel in Paris.

He diligently collected as large a number as possible of authentic writings by St Augustine, St Ambrose, St Jerome and St Gregory, and also the books of other orthodox doctors; when he had done, he himself took great pleasure in studying these, and he willingly lent the books to be studied by others. He liked better to have new copies of these works made than to buy copies already in existence, because, he said, "that the number and usefulness of these religious works were thereby increased." By his will he divided the books in this library between the Jacobins of Paris and Compiègne, the Cordeliers of Paris, and the monks of his beloved abbey of Royaumont; "and he did this," Tillemont adds, "not without probability because his son, Philip III., was not inclined to learning, although he had been taught."[1]

St Louis's acquaintance with theology and Holy Scripture, continually cultivated in these several ways, was remarkable without being altogether that of a doctor of the Church. Of this he sometimes gave an unexpected proof, for instance in the following case taken by M. Lecoy de la Marche from an unpublished sermon by Robert of Sorbon. "A learned clerk was preaching before the King of France. He spoke as follows: 'All the apostles, at the moment of the Passion, forsook Christ, and

---

[1] William of Nangis, while praising Philip III., has no hesitation in saying that he was illiterate and a little too much addicted to a purely secular life, "quamvis illiteratus et actui seculari fuerit aliquando deditus." In this respect the contrast with his father had evidently struck his contemporaries.

faith died out of their hearts; the Virgin Mary alone retained it from the day of the Passion to the day of the Resurrection; it is in memory of this that during the week of penitence at matins all the lights are put out, one after the other, save one only, reserved to light them again at Easter.' Another churchman of the highest rank then rose to reprove the preacher, and to induce him to say only what was in Scripture; he held that the apostles had forsaken Jesus Christ in body, not in heart. The preacher would have been obliged to retract in public, but the king in his turn rose and intervened. 'The assertion is not false,' he said, 'it is plainly written in the Fathers; bring me the book by St Augustine.' This was done, and the king pointed out a passage in the Gospel of St John, in which in fact the famous doctor expresses himself as follows: *Fugerunt, relicto eo corde et corpore.*"

After what we have seen, we cannot be surprised that from the twofold point of view of religion and intellect it was one of the greatest pleasures and most welcome relaxation of St Louis to converse on subjects relating to the doctrine and history of Christianity. For this reason he disliked the ceremonious festivals at which he had to receive his high barons, and preferred his habitual associates or the company of his household knights and clergy, a small number of invited guests, chiefly selected from those ecclesiastics and religious who were famed for their knowledge and virtue. Geoffrey of Beaulieu tells us that he had little taste for the scholastic method which was becoming every day more prevalent in the schools of the university of Paris, but which he doubtless regarded with suspicion because the errors with which it started were repressed by the Church, yet he honoured, when occasion served, the great minds which at that time made the method most illustrious. One of the earliest and most trustworthy biographers of St Thomas Aquinas, who as we are aware lived and taught in Paris under St Louis, has related a fact of this nature. The story is curious, and quite in agreement with the respective characters of the two saints.

"One day," writes William of Tours, "St Louis, King of France, invited the holy doctor to his table. St Thomas humbly excused himself, because he was at the moment engaged in composing his *Summary of Theology*. But at the express command of the king and of the prior of the friars of Paris, he left his work and went to the palace, his thoughts still full of the subject which had occupied him in his cell. All at once during the meal, seized with a sudden inspiration, he struck the table and exclaimed, ' Here is a decisive point against the Manichean heresy.' The prior touched him, saying, ' Be careful, master, you are at the table of the King of France '; and he pulled his robe hard, so as to rouse him from his absence of mind. The holy doctor, then coming to himself, bowed before the king and begged him to forgive him for having allowed himself to be so distracted at the royal table. But the holy king was on the contrary full of admiration and edification. He even wished to make sure that the thought by which the doctor had been so absorbed

THE MAN

should not unhappily be lost. He therefore called one of his secretaries, in order that it might instantly be written down."

This appears to us to be a charming trait, taken from nature. It may be said to complete the picture of St Louis's intellectual features, and at the same time it furnishes another instance of his constant ardour, his indefatigable and apostolic zeal.

CHAPTER VII

THE ASCETIC AND THE APOSTLE—ST LOUIS'S TRANSCENDENT VIRTUES

FAITH was the foundation of St Louis's moral and intellectual life, but love was the foundation of his sanctity. His example is such as to confirm the definition made by M. Henri Joly: "The saint is a man who serves God heroically and out of love." The love of God was his primary teaching to his son Philip and his daughter Isabel. He poured out his heart more fully to the latter, since he was aware of her more fervent piety: "Beloved daughter, I enjoin you to love our Lord God with all your heart and all your might; for without such love every one is of little worth, and nothing else can be loved so profitably. He is the Lord, to Whom every creature may say: 'Lord, Thou art my God, Who hast no need of any good thing of mine.' He is the Lord, Who sent His blessed Son on earth, and who offered Him up to death so as to deliver us from the pains of hell. Beloved daughter, if you love Him, the profit will be yours. That creature has gone far astray whose heart's love is bestowed elsewhere than on Him, or in submission to Him. Beloved daughter, the measure of the love which we should give to God is to love Him without measure. He is indeed fully entitled to our love, since He first loved us."

This ardent love explains his insatiable thirst for prayer, both in public and private, and his indefatigable assiduity in the repeated offices of divine worship. We must, especially on the latter point, take account of mediæval customs, when the piety even of laymen, and especially of kings, was of a more liturgical, and, as we may say, of a more ritual character than in our day. But, allowing for this, St Louis's devotion is not less extraordinary, and so it was regarded by the most fervent of his followers.

Queen Margaret's confessor writes as follows: "This was the pious king's custom with respect to divine service. He rose at midnight and summoned his clerks and chaplains; then they entered the chapel in the king's presence, and each night they chanted musically and aloud the matins of the day and those of our Lady; nevertheless, the pious king did not fail to repeat them in a low voice with one of his chaplains; and when matins had been said the chaplains might, if they pleased, go back to bed. And after a short space, often so short that they had not time to fall asleep again, they were called to say prime; and then they chanted prime musically and aloud, and the pious king repeated the words at the same time with one of his chaplains. And when prime had been sung, the pious king heard each day a mass for the dead. And on every Monday the pious king caused the angels' mass to be sung; on every Tuesday the mass for the Blessed Virgin Mary; on every Thursday the mass for the Holy Spirit;

on every Friday the mass of the Cross; on every Saturday again the mass for our Lady. And moreover, besides these masses, the mass for the day was daily sung. And during Lent he always heard three masses every day, one of which was said at noon or towards noon. And when he was on a journey in summer, and the heat was great, he used to ride in the early morning; but as soon as he reached his resting place he caused the usual masses to be said. When it was dinner time he went into the chapel before eating, and the chaplains sang before him tierce and sext, those for the day and those for our Lady; and he repeated the same hours in a low voice with one of his chaplains. And when he happened to be on horseback at the hour of tierce and sext, or of nona, he would cause his chaplains to sing these hours as they rode, and he himself repeated them in a low voice with one of his chaplains. And after supper the chaplains went into the chapel and sang complines with music, those of the day and those of our Lady; and the pious king when he was in his oratory often knelt down while complines were sung, and applied himself to prayer all the while. And each day after complines the chaplains sang one of the ancient melodies of our Lady, solemnly and with music, together with the prayer which ought to follow it. After this the pious king went to his chamber, and then one of his priests came; and holy water was brought and the priest sprinkled the room, saying the versicle *Asperges me*, and the prayer which should follow. And when the time came for the pious king to lie down in bed, he said the double complines with one of his chaplains. And when the pious king was in a place where there was no chapel, his chamber took the place of it, but almost everywhere in his kingdom there was a chapel. And even when the pious king was ill, the hours were solemnly sung by his chaplains in the chapel, and two other clerks or religious said the hours of the day and of our Lady beside his bed, and, unless he was too weak, he said one of the verses and the clerks the other; and when he was so weak that he could not speak, he had another clerk near him who said the verses of the psalms for him.

"On all the Sundays in Advent, and on all the festivals of the apostles, of St Nicholas, of St Martin, of St Mary Magdalene, and on similar festivals, he ordered mass to be solemnly chanted with deacon and sub-deacon. And on the solemn festivals he always liked to have one or more bishops to sing the solemn mass. And sometimes on the very great festivals, he wished the prelates to be present at the matins which he himself heard in his chapel. And on the solemn festivals of God and of our Lady, and on such like high festivals, he caused divine service to be celebrated with such solemnity and fulness that he may be said to have wearied those who took part in it, because of the length of the office. And the pious king was so resolved that divine service should be held with order and solemnity, that it did not suffice that his chaplains and clerks should arrange who should sing the mass, or who should read the gospel, or who should do the other things, but he often took order for these things himself, and sent word by one of his chaplains to those whom he considered most fit for the offices they undertook. And in order that our Saviour might be honoured in all things, he had in his chapel vestments for the priests and the other ecclesiastical orders, and vestments also for the bishops, made of samite and of other costly silken stuffs embroidered, and others of divers colours according to the season and the festival.

"Moreover, the pious king said every day the office for the dead, according to the usage of the church of Paris. Even in winter, when it was very cold, the pious king when at church or in his chapel, always stood upright on his feet, or knelt on the ground or pavement, or leaned his elbows on the bench in front of him; he seated himself on the ground without any cushion, but with only a carpet laid on the ground. While mass was said he would suffer no one to speak to him, except for some grave cause; yet sometimes, after the mass and a little before the *secrète*, he would lend an ear to his almoner, but to no one else, and only for a few moments. It often happened that he rose softly from his bed and dressed himself, and put on his shoes so swiftly in order to go more quickly to his chapel, that the attendants who lay in his chamber had no time to put on their shoes, and were forced to run after him barefoot. And when matins had been said he remained long in prayer, either in his chapel or in his wardrobe or beside his bed; and when he rose from prayer, if it was not yet daylight, he sometimes put off his robe and lay down in bed, and sometimes he lay down in his robe and fell asleep. He sometimes gave his servants a certain measure of candle and gave orders that he was only to sleep until this was burnt out; when they awoke him as they were told, and he arose, occasionally telling them that he was not yet warm, nevertheless he rose quickly and went to church or to his chapel. But since these excessive vigils and the other pains and labour which he had so long endured had greatly weakened him, some wise religious counselled him not to watch so much and not to rise so early; and after that he no longer rose at such an early hour, yet he rose soon enough for matins to be always said before daylight, at any rate in winter."

The queen's good confessor has not in the foregoing pages exhausted the inexhaustible subject of the devotion of St Louis. He returns to it again and again, and although we are unable to follow him through the infinite details, which are not without repetitions, yet we must give a few more characteristic traits.

"Without counting his other prayers, the holy king knelt down each evening fifty times, and each time he stood upright, then knelt again, and repeated slowly an Ave Maria.[1] After matins was said, the pious king remained alone in prayer before the altar, at least when he was in a place where there was a chapel; if not, he prayed beside his bed, but then

[1] This, as M. Lecoy de la Marche observes, is doubtless the devotion of the rosary.

prayers were so long that his head and his sight were weakened by them, because he bowed to the earth with his head bent, so that when he rose he did not know how to get back to bed and needed the help of one of the chamberlains who waited on him, and he would say: 'Where am I?' always in a low voice, on account of the knights who lay in his chamber. And, as the pious king's confessor tells us in the life he has written of him, the pious king was wonderfully desirous of the gift of tears, and he complained to his confessor that he could not shed tears, and told him with all simplicity and humility, that when these words of the litany were said: 'Good Lord God, we implore Thee to give us a fountain of tears,' the pious king himself said devotedly: 'Oh Lord God, I dare not ask for a fountain of tears, but a few little drops would suffice to water the dryness of my heart.' Yet he told his confessor that our Saviour sometimes accorded to him the grace of tears while he was at prayer, and when he felt them flowing softly down his face, even to his lips, they seemed to him most sweet, not only to his heart, but to the taste."[1]

St Louis maintained the vigour and depth of this love, always efficacious, if not always equally efficacious, by repairing to the flowing sources of which Jesus Christ has remitted the keeping and dispensation to the Church. He made his confession regularly on every Friday to one of his two habitual con-

[1] These tears, says St Theresa, in some sort the fruit of our efforts, sustained by divine help, are of inestimable value, and all the labours of the world would not suffice to buy one of them.

THE MAN

fessors, the one belonging to the order of St Dominic, the other to that of St Francis. His delicacy of conscience was extreme.[1] The authoritative opinion of Geoffrey of Beaulieu, expressed under an oath in the inquiry into his canonisation, states, however, that he was never guilty of a single mortal sin. He communicated with extraordinary fervour, with a penetrating humility and compunction. Queen Margaret's confessor writes:[2] "He communicated at least six times in each year, that is to say, at Easter, Pentecost, the Assumption of the Blessed Virgin, All Saints', Christmas, and the Purification of our Lady. He went to receive his Saviour with great devotion; for first he washed his hands and his mouth, took off his hood and hat, and after entering the church choir he did not walk to the altar, but went upon his knees; and when he was before the altar, he said his *confiteor* with clasped hands, with many sighs and groans, and then he received the true body of Jesus Christ from the hand of the bishop or priest."

St Louis's devotion was of an essentially Catholic character. The love of God, of God incarnate in Jesus Christ, which burned in his heart, was attached,

[1] During his last illness he refused on a Saturday to take the chicken broth ordered by the doctors, because his confessor was not there to give special permission. St Louis's firmness of mind is so well known, that these references are not of a nature to be contested. Moreover, in the Middle Ages, a somewhat excessive importance was attached to the observance of the law of abstinence.

[2] It may be conjectured that these words apply to his public communions, and that he communicated more often in his chapel in what may be called a private manner.

in accordance with human nature, to the exterior signs and tokens of the beloved object. Hence his singular veneration for relics, and especially for those relics of the Passion, of which he rejoiced to become the possessor. It was in order to preserve them in a worthy sanctuary that he built, at great cost, the *Sainte Chapelle*, that incomparable jewel of mediæval French architecture. Friday was to him a day of personal mourning, and he abstained, as far as possible, from laughing on that day. Much more did he abandon himself on Good Friday to the effusion of penitential fervour. Queen Margaret's confessor writes: "On Good Friday, each year, the pious King Louis went to visit the neighbouring churches, and he went barefoot; for this purpose he wore shoes without soles, so that the flesh might not be seen, but he placed the soles of his feet quite bare upon the ground. He made large offerings on the altars of the churches visited by him. He was present throughout the office of our Saviour, and always remained barefoot until after the adoration of the Holy Cross, and he went to adore it in this manner: he laid aside his robe and remained in his doublet or coat,[1] and thus, without belt or hood, bareheaded and barefooted, he knelt down and devoutly worshipped the Holy Cross; then he went some space forward on his knees and prayed; finally he went for the third time on his knees to the Cross and adored it; then he kissed it with great

---

[1] The coat was an under tunic with tight sleeves. The doublet only differed from the coat in being less full. The robe was a straight mantle, resting on the shoulders, and fastened on the chest by a strap or hook.

devotion and reverence, and prostrated himself in the form of the Cross to kiss it, and it is believed that he shed tears in so doing."

With the saints it is love again which takes the form of extraordinary acts of penitence connected with the sufferings endured by Jesus Christ for the sins of men. St Louis, notwithstanding his rank, was not sparing of these. His desire for fasting and abstinence was moderated by his confessors, yet it still greatly exceeded the ordinary precepts of the Church. He sought to supply by ingenious mortifications that which was forbidden to him by his rank and his weak health. Geoffrey of Beaulieu writes: "He had heard of a religious who wholly abstained from all sorts of fruit, except that when some new fruit was offered to him for the first time he would taste it as if to give thanks to God, and then abstain throughout the year. The holy king related this example to his confessor, and added with a sigh that he did not dare to try to attain to such high perfection. But it occurred to him at any rate to do the contrary, that is, when some new fruit was offered to him he would abstain from eating it the first time, so as to sacrifice the first fruits to our Lord, and after that he would eat of it with tranquillity." He did not like beer, as any one could see from his expression when he was drinking it. Wherefore he was pleased to make use of this drink during Lent. But these austerities were only trivial and he wished for such as he might feel more. If, as we have seen, he gave up the hair shirt, he did not fail to put a belt of horsehair on his flesh from time to time.

Every Friday, after his confession, he had himself scourged by his confessor with a discipline made of five iron chains, and when he found that the good confessor set about it too gently, he made a sign to him to strike harder. It is true that he once told Geoffrey of Beaulieu that the zeal of one of the predecessors of this good Dominican needed no encouragement, for his mode of action in such case, of which the pious king had never complained to him, did not precisely err in respect of want of vigour.

With the saints acts of penitence are the fruit of love, and this is still more the case with acts of charity. "Pity," Queen Margaret's confessor writes, "so filled and transported the holy king's heart that he seemed to abandon himself altogether to the sick and poor," and he gives a proof of this in the long enumeration of St Louis's good works, which would fill too many pages. His expenditure in such acts was profuse. We must content ourselves with the account of his habitual alms-giving given by M. Wallon, one of his best biographers: "Every day the king sent for a hundred and twenty-two poor people, and gave to each two loaves, worth a Parisian *denier*, a measure of wine, meat or fish according to the season, and a Parisian *denier*; and if there was a woman in the throng who had one or more children, as many loaves were given to her as she had children, a loaf for each child. Sixty other poor people received their bread in money, that is to say, four *deniers* a piece, twice a week. All the poor, whencesoever they came, had what was left from his table; the almoner had orders to add as much bread as was

THE MAN

needful, so that no one might go away empty-handed; and his alms were increased with the scarcity of bread and with poverty. When he went to Berry, to Normandy, or to any other place not generally frequented by him, it was of the poor that he first thought. He would cause the assembly of three hundred at a time in order to distribute alms; and he may be said to have gone on his way doing good. He sometimes went on a journey in order to see and feed the poor. He would say to his attendants, 'Let us go to visit the poor of such a district, and feed them.'"

St Louis's love of Jesus Christ, thoroughly infused with the teachings and precepts of the Gospel, drew him to the miserable as to the representatives and substitutes on earth of God incarnate. Therefore he did not think that he had done enough by alms-giving, and it was his custom and delight to add more definite acts of personal service. In this he found the precious gain of satisfying at once his threefold ardour of charity, humility and penitence. "On feast days," continues M. Wallor, on the authority of contemporary accounts, "he assembled two hundred poor in his palace, and himself served at the meal. On Wednesdays, Fridays and Saturdays in Advent and Lent, and on Wednesdays and Fridays throughout the year, he caused thirteen to come into his chamber or to the adjoining room, and fed them with his own hand, without being repelled by their uncleanliness. If one of the number was blind, the king put the piece of bread in one hand, and guided the other to the vessel containing his pittance. If it happened to be fish, the king took out the bones, dipped the morsel in the sauce, and put it in the blind man's mouth. Before the meal he gave to each twelve *deniers*, or more, according to their need; when a woman had a child with her, he gave also for the child. On Saturdays he took the three most miserable and infirm of the number and led them into his wardrobe, where were three troughs of water, with linen; he washed their feet, then dried and devoutly kissed them, however disfigured they might be and worn by constant friction; then he knelt to offer them water to wash their hands, and gave them forty *deniers*, and kissed their hands. Nor was this all; every day and in all weather he caused thirteen other poor people to come to him, and he chose the three most revolting from the thirteen to sit at a table spread beside him. He gave them forty *deniers*, and caused three vessels to be brought in which he himself undertook to prepare their soup; he cut up the meat and fish which was put before him, and gave it to them. Moreover, as if still better to confound our delicacy, he caused the meat which had been served to them to be brought back, and ate after them. One day he saw an aged man among these three poor people who ate little. He caused the vessel full of food to be set before him, and when the old man had eaten as much as he liked, the king took and tasted it after him; honouring Jesus Christ in this poor and aged man, and esteeming what he had left good enough for himself.

As the Saviour had washed his disciples' feet, after

the Supper, he liked to do the same, literally obeying the divine precept. On Holy Thursday, authorised by the Saviour's example, he was not afraid to do it before his Court. On that holy day he washed the feet of thirteen poor men, and gave them forty *deniers*. Afterwards, when his sons were with him, he caused them to do the same. And it was not a mere ceremony, as we see it to-day in the ritual of this holy day. On one occasion, one of the old men, taking the king's office seriously and wishing to take advantage of it, observed that the inside of his toes was not clean and begged him in all simplicity to cleanse them. Those who were present were angry with the boor who claimed such service of a king. But the pious king justified the demand, humbly did as the old man desired, washed and dried his toes, and added the kiss of charity."

St Louis's transcendent charity was subject to simple and sublime impulses. Such is the beautiful and picturesque episode of the Compiègne leper, told by Queen Margaret's confessor: "The pious king was at the Castle of Compiègne on Good Friday; he went barefoot on his usual pilgrimage to the churches of the town, and he went by the common road, followed by his sergeants with money in their hands to serve for the king's alms, and he often took coins from them to give to the poor whom he met, more or less according to their needs. Now as the pious king was passing along a street in this manner, a leper on the other side of the way, so ill that he could scarcely speak, rang his bell loudly in accordance with the rule, so that the passers-by might keep away, for fear of the contagion of his leprosy. Then the king, thus warned, perceived him and went towards him, for this purpose setting his feet in the cold, muddy water which ran in the middle of the street; he joined the leper, gave alms to him, and kissed his hand. There was a great press of people, and many of those who were near the pious king crossed themselves, and said one to the other, 'Look what the king has done. He has kissed the leper's hand.'"

In St Louis's eyes the unhappy man had a twofold claim to this homage: he was poor and diseased. His devotion to the suffering was one of the most marked features of the great king's piety. In his frequent visits to hospitals he took pleasure in personal ministry to the sick, and with calm humility refrained from the slightest display of repugnance. The author just quoted writes: "When some were more ill than others, he was the more ready to wait on them, and kneeling before them he cut up their bread and meat, placed the morsel all ready cut in their mouths, and then wiped them with the napkin which he carried. Some of the sick were so disgusting that the pious king's officers were revolted and withdrew backwards, and sometimes they could not abide in the place because the air was so foul and the stench from the sick so abominable, yet he would remain there as if conscious of nothing."

One day he was in the hospital at Compiègne, and looking round he saw a sick man who had what is called the disease of St Eloi in two places on his face. The pious king then sat down on the sick man's bed, peeled a pear for him, and with his own hand put the morsels in his mouth; and while doing this the matter issuing from the sick man's wounds, on each side of the nose, fell on the pious king's hand, so that the pious king had to wash his hands twice before the said sick man had finished eating the pear. At the hospital at Vernon, where he was also often at work, a touching tradition has been established and transmitted from one generation to another. It is said that he left his royal dwelling at night, and came without the knowledge of any of his attendants to lie among the sick and poor. The bed which he used was kept and pointed out, and it was called the bed of St Louis.[1]

The religious were regarded by him as representatives of Jesus Christ in a twofold sense, as consecrated to God, and as willingly poor. It was therefore a joy to him to find himself in their midst, and his joy was sometimes redoubled by taking on himself some of the humblest offices of the convent. "The pious king went often to the abbey of Royaumont, and many times, especially on a Friday or Saturday, he ate at the abbot's table in the refectory, and when this was the case he always furnished the convent with bread and wine, and four dishes of fish; at that time there were almost a hundred monks in the abbey, without counting about forty lay brothers. And on other days, when the pious king did not eat in the refectory, he was accustomed to go in, and

[1] This tradition is given by William Pépin, a celebrated Dominican preacher of the sixteenth century in one of his sermons on St Louis.

when the monks were seated at table he might be seen serving with the brothers who performed this office. He went to the kitchen window to receive the dishes of food, and bore and set them before the monks seated at table; and as there were many monks and few servers, he went to and fro with the dishes until all the convent was served. And when the dishes were too hot, he wrapped his hands in his robe, and the food was sometimes spilled upon it; and when the abbot said that he was spoiling his robe, the pious king would answer, 'It matters little. I have others.'"

In the case of sick religious his charity may be said to have been unlimited. A sister of the hospital at Vernon once, during an illness, had the whim of refusing to eat anything unless the king came to feed her with his own hands; "and when this became known to the pious king, he went to the bed where she lay and fed her, putting the morsels into her mouth with his own hands." But that which exceeds all the rest is the perfectly authentic history of the holy king's relations with Brother Léger of the abbey of Royaumont. "There was in the abbey of Royaumont a monk called Brother Léger, a deacon of the Cistercian order. He was a leper, and lived apart from the others. Owing to his disease, his state had become disgusting and horrible; his eyes were so bad that he could not see, he had lost his nose, his lips were swelled and cracked, and his eyelids were red and hideous to behold. Now the pious king came to the said abbey one day before the feast of St Remy, and according to his custom heard several masses. The Count of Flanders and other great lords were with him. When the masses were over he left the church, and on entering the infirmary approached the place assigned to the leprous monk. He ordered one of his officers to keep back his followers, and then took with him the abbot of Royaumont and told him that he intended to visit the leprous monk, whom he had formerly seen. The abbot went first, the pious king followed, and they entered the sick man's cell and found him about to eat some pork at a small table, for in this abbey it is not the custom for lepers to abstain from flesh meat. The holy king saluted the sick man, and asked how he was; then he knelt before him, and while thus kneeling he began to cut up the meat with the knife which was on the table, and he put the morsels in the sick man's mouth, who received them from the king's hand and ate them. And the abbot, out of respect for the king, also knelt at the feet of the sick man, yet not without disgust. Then the pious king asked the leper if he would not like to eat partridge or chicken, and he answered yes; then the king sent the monk in charge of the sick for one of his officers, and ordered chickens and partridges to be brought from his own kitchen, which was some way off, and all the while that the officer took to go and return the king remained upon his knees and the abbot with him. Two roast chickens and three roast partridges were brought, and the king asked the leper which he would have, chicken or partridge, and he answered partridge; and the king asked with what seasoning, and he answered, with salt; and then the pious king cut off the wings of a partridge, salted the morsels, and put them one by one into the sick man's mouth. But since the leper's lips were cracked, as we have said, the salt made them bleed, and matter issued from them and flowed on to his chin. The sick man therefore said that the salt hurt him too much, and then the king continued to dip the morsels in salt to give them taste, but he removed the grains of salt from each morsel, so that none might enter the cracks of the leper's lips. The king next asked the leper if he wished to drink, and he said yes; and he asked what wine he had, and he answered that it was good; and then the pious king, taking the flagon of wine from the table, himself poured it into the cup, and put the cup to the leper's lips and made him drink. When the meal was finished, the pious king besought the sick man to pray to our Saviour for him, and went out with the abbot, and went himself to eat at the hostel he had in the abbey. He often visited this leprous monk, and would say to his knights: 'Let us go to see our sick man.' Once when he came again during his meal, the pious king poured out the soup and gave it to him, putting the wooden spoon to his lips; but he had put too much salt in the soup, so that the sick man's lips began to bleed. One of those present said to the king, 'You have made his mouth bleed by putting too much salt in the soup,' and the pious king answered, 'I did it for him as I should have done it for myself,' and he asked the leper to pardon him."

His charity, so ardent for the sick, was as great for the dead. He was deeply concerned for the succour of their souls, seeking and finding ingenious methods of procuring for them more abundant prayers. He also occupied himself with the interests of those who died while causes were pending before him, saying that people were too apt to favour the living at their expense. When he was in the Holy Land, he manifested with an altogether transcendent heroism his devotion to the lifeless remains of those whom he regarded as having given their lives for the faith. After a sharp attack made by the Saracens upon Sidon, which the king was engaged in fortifying, more than two thousand corpses were left on the sea shore and in adjacent places. St Louis's first care when he came to this city to repair the disaster was to provide in person for their burial. M. Wallon writes: " He caused a cemetery to be consecrated, in which great trenches were dug, and in order that no one might recoil from the disgust and danger of the task, he himself collected the corpses and placed them on the cloths which had been sewn together in order to place them on camels or horses and bear them to the trenches. Many of his household followed him who had not the heart to do the like, and they held their noses while the king simply went on with the work without seeming to be conscious of the foul emanations of the place. Putrefaction had gone so far that in laying hold of the dead by the arm or leg the limb remained in the hand. The king even collected the entrails which were scattered on the soil. This labour lasted for four or five days. Each morning after mass the pious king set to work again, saying to the others, ' Let us go to bury our martyrs'; and when many appeared to go unwillingly, he added: 'They have suffered death, we may also suffer somewhat'; and again, 'Do not be revolted by these bodies, for they are martyrs and in Paradise.' The archbishop of Tyre, the bishop of Damietta, and another bishop stood beside the trenches for the burial, reciting the office for the dead, and the king with them; these three prelates kept aloof as far as possible from the pestilential odour, but not so the king. The archbishop of Tyre died two days later, and the two other bishops became seriously ill. Men said, and it may be true, that it was owing to this infection."

Christian faith, animated to this degree by love, might, and indeed did, make an apostle of St Louis. His example alone was a continual apostolate. But, as we have already seen, he wished and knew how to work more directly for the salvation of his family, of his friends and of all his followers. On those who were more remote from him he did not fail to exert, when occasion served, the personal effect of a salutary exhortation. This is shown, besides other instances, by an interesting story told by William of Chartres: "It once happened at a royal court of justice that a lady, whose affair had just been settled, entered the king's chamber with some other persons, adorned with excessive elegance. The king specially noted her presence. She had, in fact, according to the vain judgment of the world, been formerly famous for her brilliant beauty. The king, in his devotion to God, then conceived the thought of familiarly exhorting this lady on the subject of her salvation. He called brother Geoffrey, who was present, and said to him: 'Stay with me, you shall hear what I propose to say to the lady you see there, and who seeks to speak to me.' Having therefore, as it seemed good to him, sent away the other persons present, the king, left alone with the lady and with brother Geoffrey, spoke thus to the lady: 'Madame, I desire to recall to your mind a thing which concerns your salvation. It is said that you were formerly a very fair lady, but what was formerly is now past, as you are aware. You may therefore easily see that this beauty was vain and useless, since it has vanished so quickly, just as a flower which has scarcely opened fades and does not endure, and with all your care and diligence you cannot cause it to return. Now, therefore, you must provide yourself with another beauty, not of the body, but of the soul, wherewith to please God, our Creator, and make amends for the negligence of your conduct in the time of your vanished beauty.' The lady listened patiently to this exhortation, and afterwards corrected herself and adopted habits of greater propriety and modesty."

St Louis's zealous apostolate extended to all his subjects. William of Chartres writes: " In the government of his kingdom he was not only careful and anxious about the care of their bodies and of their material interests, which is the strict duty of a king, and one which he observed day and night, but by a holy extension of this duty, and as it were by a pious usurpation, he was moved to an incredible degree by the desire of saving their souls, on which he was so intent that he might be said to use his kingship as if it were a priesthood." It was for this reason, as well as from piety and charity, that he lavished his favour and benefits on the religious orders, and showed special affection for the two great organs of renovation and conversion with which the Church had been recently and successively enriched, and to which the Catholic revival of the thirteenth century was due; the sons of St Francis and the sons of St Dominic; the minor, and the preaching friars. He said to his friends with graceful humour, that if he could divide his body in two, he would give half to one, half to the other of these orders. Justice and honesty were, however, even more to him than charity itself, and the apostolate. Joinville writes: "He said that it was an evil thing to take the goods of others, for to restore them is so hard that even the utterance of the word flays the throat because of the *r's* that are in it; and these are the devil's rakes, since he always holds back those who wish to restore the goods of others. And the devil does this with subtlety, for in the case of great usurers and great robbers, he impels them to give to God that which they ought to restore to man. He bade me tell the king Thibaut from him to be careful lest in founding at Provins the house of the preaching friars, he should do hurt to his soul by the large sums with which he endowed it. For wise men ought, in their lifetime, to use their goods as testamentary executors ought to do; that is, good executors first satisfy the claims made on the dead, and restore the goods of others, and give alms out of what remains."

To his care for the saving of Christian souls St Louis added an ardent desire for the conversion of the unbelieving. He laboured, not without success, for the conversion of the Jews. M. Lecoy de la Marche writes: "An account of the year 1261 shows that twenty-four baptised Jews each received fourteen *deniers* daily from the royal treasury. The king liked to give to his proselytes the names of Louis, Louis of Poissy, and Blanche, and doubtless answered for them at the font." The triumph of which he dreamed in his crusades was not merely the defeat of the Saracens, but the adhesion of most of them to the religion of Jesus Christ. M. Lecoy de la Marche says: "He took with him a pacific troop of preaching and minor friars, who were constantly occupied in preaching the gospel to unbelievers. During his stay at Saint John of Acre, these religious, according to Primat's chronicle, converted five hundred Turks or Arabs; from this we can judge of what they may have done in the course of the crusade. Geoffrey of Beaulieu and the queen's confessor also speak of a number of baptised Saracens, ransomed and brought to France by the king's care; they were maintained at his expense, he caused them to marry Christian women and their families remained under his care." His saintly concern for the apostolate clearly prompted his answer to Joinville with respect to the rumour that the Saracens, after the murder of their soldan, thought of putting their royal prisoner in his place.

"The king was told that the emirs were very desirous to make him soldan of Babylon. And he asked me if I thought that he would have taken the kingdom of Babylon if it had been offered to him. And I said to him that he would have acted as a madman, since they had slain their lord; and he told me that he should not have refused it." One of his chief reasons for conducting his second crusade to Tunis was the idea suggested by what was in fact illusory information, that the sovereign of the country was disposed to be converted if he could be secured from the danger of such an act. "Oh!" St Louis exclaimed in his apostolic zeal, "if I could but see myself the sponsor of such a godson." He sought to prepare the way for this pacific triumph by causing the ambassadors of the Mussulman prince to be present at the conversion of a famous Jew, for whom the king stood sponsor, with several great nobles, at the church of St Denis. When the ceremony was over, the ambassadors of the king of Tunis were called before him and he said with fervour, "Tell the king your master from me that my desire for the saving of his soul is so strong that I would spend the rest of my life in a Saracen prison and never more see the light of the sun, if only your king and his people would become Christian from the depths of the heart."

The pious king had an occasion to extend his apostolate beyond the Saracens as far as the Mongol Tartars, and he did not fail to make use of it. Joinville writes: "At the time when the king was in Cyprus, the great king of the Tartars sent messengers to him with many friendly and civil words.[1] Among other things, he sent word that he was ready to help him to conquer the Holy Land, and to deliver Jerusalem from the hands of the Saracens. The king received these messengers with great courtesy, and sent messengers of his own, who remained two years before they returned. And the king sent by his messengers a tent fashioned like a chapel, which was very costly, for it was all made of good and fine scarlet stuff. And in order to see if he could draw this people to our faith, the king caused carvings to be made for the said chapel of the Annunciation of our Lady, of the Nativity and the Baptism of our Saviour, of the Passion, the Ascension, and the coming of the Holy Spirit, together with chalices, books, and all which is needful for the singing of mass, and two preaching friars who knew the Saracen tongue, in order to show and teach them what to believe."

This attempt had no result, and Joinville tells us that when St Louis was informed on the return of his embassy of the great Khan's real opinions, he regretted having sent it. If the holy king's clear mind and solid judgment were sometimes subject to illusion and chimera, it was assuredly due to his apostolic zeal. It is certain that if he could with a safe conscience have laid down his crown in order to go himself in the habit of a preaching or minor

[1] M. Wallon observes that this was not the successor of Genghis-Khan, but apparently one of his officers in Asia, who sent a deputation to St Louis, in order to enter into friendly relations with him. It is not impossible that this officer was a Nestorian, who flattered the king with the hope of converting his people.

friar on a mission to the Tartars, he would have held such a change of station to be not only a great honour, but a great joy. Setting aside the idea of a mission, the positive assertion of his confessor, Geoffrey of Beaulieu, already mentioned by us, does not allow us to doubt that at one period of his life he seriously thought of giving up the throne to his son, in order to make his profession in one of the two great orders which were so dear to him. It is so far from correct to say that no other saint was more of a layman than Louis, that, on the contrary, while he remained in the world and in possession of power, and fulfilled his duty, he satisfied his monastic tastes and inclinations as far as possible, and took pleasure in the smallest details of religious life. In his frequent visits to Royaumont, as we are told by Queen Margaret's confessor, "it often happened that when the abbot and monks entered the church to say complines, the pious king was with them like one of the monks; when complines were ended and, according to custom in this order, the abbot stepped before the others, distributing holy water from the receptacle beside the dormitory door, to each in order, then they bowed one after the other and went up to the dormitory to lie down, and then the pious king often remained beside the abbot who thus gave holy water to each one, and he devoutly watched all that was done; and he received holy water from the said abbot like one of the monks, and, after bowing the head, he left the cloister and went to his hostel, and all this was done by the king in the presence of many of his household."

THE MAN

It was in this direction that his heart inclined more and more, in spite of his strong and deep affection for the queen and his children. But his duty was elsewhere, and when reminded of this he sacrificed his inclination, and in a certain sense his piety, or, as we should rather say, he continued to seek in the accomplishment of his duty, made heavier, yet sanctified by the sacrifice, the first and chief exercise of this piety, nourished by faith and love. As Bourdaloue says: " It is the happiness of these glorious saints that they have never separated their perfection from their duty, or, as we should rather say, they have known no other perfection but that which was connected with their duty. St Louis is numbered with those whom we invoke to-day, because, being a king, he nobly fulfilled the duties of a king, because he was a saintly king. You have only to consult his history to admit this truth." The kingship was indeed a burden to St Louis, although it was his fit and full vocation. We have now to see how he bore and exercised the office.

II. THE KING

CHAPTER I

THE KNIGHT AND THE COMMANDER—ST LOUIS'S FIRST WARS

MILITARY qualities and personal bravery, at all times of importance to sovereigns, were in the thirteenth century still absolutely necessary for a king. In addition to his religious, moral and literary education, facts clearly show that St Louis had been instructed in the duties of chivalry and war, like other princes and great lords of his time. Moreover, from the time of his accession to the throne, at the age of twelve years, he was in this respect subject to the lessons of practical experience, since he accompanied the energetic Queen Regent in her successive expeditions against the revolted barons. At the age of fifteen he assumed the command of the royal army for the first time in person, under Queen Blanche's eye; the campaign directed in January 1229 against Peter Mauclerc, Count of Brittany, was inaugurated by the siege of the castle of Bellême in Perche, a fortress reputed to be impregnable. This important enterprise, accomplished in mid-winter, was full of instruction for him.

According to M. Elie Berger's interesting account: " Blanche of Castile did not only accompany her son, but had an eye to everything, and attended to the welfare and subsistence of the army. As the cold was excessive, she caused great fires to be lighted where the horses were picquetted, so that they might not suffer from the frost; she promised wages to all those who would go into the forest and about the country to cut down trees and bring into camp the wood which was required; in this way not only the king's quarters and those of the marshal were warmed, but the soldiers' tents. The camp followers requisitioned waggons, and fulfilled this task. The approaches of a siege at that time involved a large quantity of wood; the forest trees were cut down, and the houses of Bellême and Sérigny were demolished, in order that the beams might be used, and stones procured for discharging in the machines of war.

"On the day following the first assault, which was vigorously repulsed, the marshal sent miners to the front and ordered them to sap the foundations of the castle, while he covered their work with his troop of knights. At the same time the attack was resumed everywhere; the garrison made a brave response to the onslaught of the assailants; the miners were compelled to fall back, and then to fly; but at the end of the rude conflict, which lasted until three o'clock in the afternoon, the base of the ramparts was much damaged. On the following day, in the morning, the marshal had two machines prepared, one of which hurled large, and the other small stones against the walls. The first of these machines finally sent such an enormous projectile into the interior of the fortress that the commander's dwelling fell in upon the people who were in it, and at the same time the keep tottered on its foundations and was shattered. The garrison then lost courage; they saw no relief at hand; the walls which they had bravely defended were partly mined, and half destroyed in their upper part; the soldiers of Peter Mauclerc capitulated, and the king pardoned them."

St Louis was no longer a child, and actually held the reins of power in his hands, when at the age of twenty-eight (1242), he had to decide on and to conduct the important war against the Count de la Marche and the king of England, who was the ally of this rebellious vassal. His moral and material preparation was excellent. The laborious endeavours of Henry III. only procured the co-operation of the English barons to an insufficient extent, while the king of France, by a clear and firm explanation of his rights and intentions, rallied his nobles to his side. He assembled and grouped his forces with order and vigour. "He had collected," says M. Faure, one of his best historians, "as large a number as possible of artisans, and ordered them to construct moveable machines, mangonels, castles upon wheels, and moveable barbicans, such as would facilitate an approach to the walls and permit an attack at close quarters, since he was about to undertake a war of sieges in a district full of castles held by the rebels. He had got together a large store of provisions, as well as materials for constructing camps. He had ordered the communal forces to make like provision of stores, and to bring ladders and waggons. Provisions,

THE KING

German sword in his hand." He is, as we can see, no longer the "monk" so admired by the friar Salimbene in the Franciscan convent at Sens. His calmness did not hinder him from displaying at the given moment a useful valour. Joinville goes on with the story: "It was said that we should have been altogether lost that day, but for the king in person. For the sire of Courtenay and John of Saillenay told me that six Turks had seized the king's horse's rein by the bridle in order to take him prisoner, and he was delivered by himself alone, striking them hard with his sword. And when the soldiers saw how the king defended himself, they took courage, and many of them ceased to cross the stream and came to the king's aid." The Christian army remained in possession of the field, and in the evening occupied the Saracen camp itself.

The king immediately took excellent measures in order to profit by the only effective result of his victory, that of making himself master of both sides of the canal. He hastened to throw a wooden bridge across it, and to establish several bridges of boats to maintain the connection between his troops and those which occupied his former camp; the machines of the Saracens which remained in his possession were broken up and used to surround his position with barricades. But the hostile army was far from being destroyed or discouraged. It was encamped at a little distance, still covering Mansourah, under the command of Fakr-eddin's successor, Bibars-Bondocdar. On the following Friday, February 11, he took the offensive and directed a furious attack on the crusaders, which was repelled with great difficulty. "After the battle," says Joinville, "the king summoned all his barons before him and said, 'We owe thanks to our Lord who has given us great honour twice in this week, first on Shrove Tuesday, when we drove them from the camp which we now occupy, and then on Friday, when we defended ourselves against them, we being on foot and they on horseback.' And he spoke many other noble words in order to encourage them." He had given proofs in this battle of a remarkable capacity and of the most resolute valour. An eye-witness tells us "that it plainly appeared from his countenance that he had in his heart neither terror, nor fear, nor emotion."

Unfortunately the losses sustained by the Christian army obliged it to remain from henceforth on the defensive, always a perilous thing in the midst of an enemy's country. The Saracens, encouraged by the arrival of their new sultan, Touran-Chah, who made his entry into Mansourah on the 27th February to the sound of cymbals and drums, which were heard in the christian camp, were full of ardour and hope. With a bold strategy which determined the issue of the campaign, they transported large boats on the backs of camels into the canal Mehallet-Kebir; this canal, by a secondary branch, joined the Nile below the crusaders' camp, and part of the christian flotilla was attacked on both sides, taken, and destroyed. Thus masters of the course of the stream, the enemy cut the chief communication with Damietta and intercepted all convoys. A terrible epidemic of scurvy and dysentery, aggravated by famine, broke out in the army; St Louis was also attacked, but he did not cease to sustain the courage of others by his heroic firmness and superhuman serenity. He opened negotiations with the young Sultan which came to nothing. He was obliged to decide to re-cross the Thanis, and, notwithstanding the attacks of the enemy, the first movement in retreat was executed in admirable order, although his own condition and that of the army rendered it very difficult.[1]

But every day the mortality increased, and very soon it was necessary to retreat in force. St Louis's first care was to embark the sick and unarmed people on the vessels which remained at his disposal. He threw overboard the stores and provisions kept for the use of his household in these vessels, so as to afford more room for these unfortunate people. His brothers and the legate pressed him to go on board himself, but he refused, even with vehemence. The testimony of Charles of Anjou on this point must be given. "The king dismounted from his horse and stood leaning against the saddle, surrounded by his familiar knights, Geoffrey of Sargnes, John Foinon, John of Valery, Peter of Bauçay, Robert of Bazoches, and Gaucher of Châtillon, who, seeing his serious illness and the danger to which he exposed himself by remaining on land, began to implore him, all and severally, to save his life by going on board a ship. He always refused to forsake his people. King Charles, his

[1] Charles of Anjou deposes that the king's condition became worse on the very night of the retreat, and that, in addition to other maladies, diarrhœa compelled him to dismount several times.

brother, at that time Count of Anjou, said to him, 'Sire, you do wrong in resisting the good advice given by your friends, and in refusing to go on board a ship; for if you remain on land there may be a dangerous delay in the march of the army, and you may be the cause of our destruction.' And he said this, as he afterwards reported, with the desire of saving the king, fearing so greatly to lose him that he would have given all his heritage and that of his children to know that the king was in Damietta. But the king, deeply moved, replied with a wrathful countenance, 'Count of Anjou, Count of Anjou! if I am a burden to you, get rid of me, but I will never forsake my people.'"

Always full of presence of mind, the heroic king had ordered the bridges of boats which united the two banks of the Thanis to be destroyed by breaking their fastenings. The army was in such confusion that this order was not executed. The Saracens crossed the canal and incessantly harassed the retreat, which soon became disastrous. Always occupied with the noble thought that he was responsible for the safety of his soldiers rather than they for his, St Louis had sent on the army corps which formed the centre, and placed himself in the rear-guard. He was, however, so weak that he could not bear the weight of his armour, and he went forward wearing a silken mantle, on a small Arab horse. On reaching a village which the Arabs call Minié-Abou-Abdallah he could go no further. He was taken off his horse and was taken into a house, where he lay like a dead man on the knees of a woman from Paris who chanced to be there. Meanwhile Gaucher of Châtillon remained outside to defend the house and died the heroic death which has been mentioned above. Although St Louis was almost at the point of death he had not lost his accustomed judgment. He authorised Philip of Montfort to negotiate a truce with the enemy, in which he was unfortunately hindered by the ill-advised intervention of a man-at-arms, who exclaimed with mistaken zeal, "Noble knights, surrender, the king commands it. Do not cause the king to be slain." The knights laid down their arms and the king himself, with his brothers, was forced to surrender to the emir Gemal-eddin. "Owing to the resistance of the rear-guard," writes M. Wallon, "the van of the army was able to go as far as Farescour, but the Saracens did not allow them to reach Damietta. After a hot conflict they also were defeated, and all those who did not perish were made prisoners; the oriflamme fell into the hands of the victors with the other standards."

St Louis's christian heroism during his captivity struck his fierce conquerors with admiration and filled them with respect, as we have already seen; his indomitable calmness was put to the test both before and after the murder of the Sultan Touran-Chah by the rebellious emirs. His kingly heroism was no less remarkable. He deliberated, negotiated, and came to a decision with the same mature reflection and perfect freedom of mind while in the hands of his enemies as if he had been in his palace in the city of Paris, peaceably surrounded by his knights and clergy. His two chief cares were the general interests of Christianity and the deliverance of the poor captives. He had this latter question much at heart. Queen Margaret's confessor writes: "When the pious king was captured by the Saracens, and many great lords with him, he heard it said that many rich christians were negotiating to pay a ransom for their delivery; but he expressly forbade them to do this, even with menaces, for fear the deliverance of the poor should be hindered by it, for he said that by this proceeding the rich would be set free and the poor, who had not wherewithal to pay ransom, would remain captives. 'But,' said he, 'leave this negotiation to me alone, for I will not permit any one to pay for his deliverance out of his own means, but I will myself undertake the ransom of all, and I will not treat for my own freedom save with all those who came with me.'" He very unwillingly consented to surrender Damietta, and only after he was assured by certain information that it was impossible to hold the town for any time against the Saracens. With respect to money, on the other hand, he was very free, and uttered a fine saying on this occasion, which Joinville has preserved for us and which shows that his humility as an ascetic took nothing from the legitimate and patriotic sense of his dignity as king of France and heir to the crown of Clovis and of Charlemagne. "The king said and promised to the emirs that he would willingly pay the five hundred thousand livres for the deliverance of his followers, and Damietta for the deliverance of his own person, since he was not such an one as ought to be ransomed with money. When the soldan heard this he said, 'By my faith, the Frank is liberal since he does not bargain about such a large sum of money.' When the time came to execute the treaty and the Saracen chiefs demanded hostages, St Louis agreed to remain alone in their hands as a hostage for the whole of the army, and it was difficult to induce him to alter this resolution. 'I wish to remain,' he said, 'and to wait until payment is made and the others are set free.'"

The same self-denial, at once truly christian and truly king-like, together with ardent zeal and steadfast judgment, are shown by his prolonging his stay in the Holy Land for four whole years after the Egyptian disaster, and his subsequent release. Joinville tells us the motives for this resolution, as he explained them to the assembled lords. "My lords, I render thanks to those who have advised me to go back to France, and I thank those also who have advised me to remain. But I am of opinion that if I remain there is no danger of any loss to my kingdom, for the queen (Blanche of Castile) has men enough for its defence, and I have also considered what the barons of this country have told me, that if I go, the kingdom of Jerusalem is lost, and that no one will dare to remain after me. I have, therefore, considered that at no price would I cause the loss of the kingdom of Jerusalem, which I have come to keep and to conquer, so my resolution is such that I have remained up to this time." Another reason which weighed most strongly with St Louis, and which he gave in the noble letter written from Saint

John of Acre in August 1250, was the deliverance of the poor captives who remained in Egypt, exposed to every danger, in consequence of the violation of the treaty by the Saracens. "The Christian prisoners retained by the unbelievers might be considered as lost after our departure, since all hope of obtaining their release would be taken away." The Christian hero's soul, saintly, royal and patriotic, breathes for us in this official report of his Egyptian campaign. His sublime calmness is apparent in the simple recital of his acts; the sincere avowal of his reverses, and his humble and confident submission to the divine will are expressed with a composed and steadfast ease, in Latin which is remarkable for the period, by the clerk who held the pen under the very present and apparent dictation of St Louis. The letter ends with a burst of enthusiastic exhortation, in which we discern the spirit of the Gospel and of the *Chanson de Roland*.

"Courage, therefore, soldiers of Christ; arm yourselves, show that your valour is able to chastise these insults and affronts of the unbelievers. Follow the example of your forefathers, specially zealous among all the nations for upholding the faith, renowned for their obedience, their devotion, their affection for their sovereigns, who filled the world with the fame of their exploits. We have preceded you in the service of God; come now to join us. Although you come late, you will out of the beneficence of our Lord receive with us the recompense which the householder in the Gospel gave not only to the first labourers in the vineyard, but to the last. . . . And

THE KING

you, prelates and other servants of Christ, invoke the Most High for us and for the Holy Land with special fervour and insistence; cause prayers to be said with this intention in all the places which are subject to you, so that the happy issue which has been hindered by our sins may by your prayers be obtained from the divine mercy and goodness."

The character of this document presents an instructive contrast with the celebrated *bulletins*, undoubtedly heroic, but too frequently exaggerated and untrue, which were issued by the great commander whose genius and fortune dominated France and the world at the beginning of this century, but whose glory, in addition to the spots by which it was stained, was fundamentally vitiated by an incurable egoism. From a military point of view Napoleon has criticised St Louis's conduct in the expedition to Egypt to his own advantage. It would be useless to deny that in the brilliant but ephemeral conquest of that country he himself displayed a superior strategy and activity, singularly aided, however, by the much greater flexibility and docility of the men whom he commanded. Yet the final failure was the same, and how different was the heroism of the two leaders. The one sacrificing all and every one with lavish indifference to the loss of life in order to attain his object, which was in the first place the satisfaction of his personal ambition, and ending by furtively abandoning his army in order to cross the sea alone and achieve the conquest of supreme power. The other always ready to sacrifice himself, as in fact he did sacrifice himself with a calm and resolute will, to the interests of the crusade and of the Holy Land, and to the safety of his soldiers. Henry Houssaye an historian rather biassed in favour of Napoleon, says of him: " He was not a man to sacrifice himself." St Louis was in the highest degree such a man, and for this reason his glory is far more pure, true and substantial than that of Napoleon.

When his conscience permitted him to return to France, he displayed another mark of devotion which, as Joinville says, " caused him yet again to put his body in peril of death in order to save his people from hurt." Let us hear the good Seneschal. "This was when we returned from across the sea, and were off the Isle of Cyprus. The vessel struck on a rock so violently that several feet of the keel were carried away. After this the king sent for fourteen master navigators, both from his own vessel and from others in his company, to advise him what to do. All were of opinion that he ought to go on board another vessel, for they did not see how this vessel could endure the shock of the waves, since the nails which fasten the planks together were all displaced. And they gave the king an instance of the perilous state of the vessel, since on our outward voyage a vessel in similar case had perished, and when I was with the count of Joigny I saw the woman and child who escaped alone from that vessel. . . . Then the king said to the navigators, 'I ask you on your honour whether you would leave this ship if it was your own, and if it was laden with your merchandise.' And they all answered No, since they would rather run the risk of being drowned than of losing a vessel worth more than four thousand livres. 'And why, then, do you advise me to disembark?' 'Because,' said they, 'the game is not equal, for neither gold nor silver can buy the price of your person, and of that of your wife and children who are here; and for this reason we advise you not to put yourself and them in peril.' The king then said, 'Sirs, I have heard your opinion and the opinion of my followers; now, I will in my turn give you mine, which is that if I leave the ship there are now five hundred people and more who will remain in the Isle of Cyprus, for there is no one who does not love his life as much as I love mine, and who, as it may chance, will never return to their country. Therefore I would rather trust my person and my wife and children to the hand of God than do so much hurt to the large number of people now there.'"

St Louis's second crusade, undertaken when he was in a deplorable state of health, twenty-two years after the first, was certainly a great act of earthly self-denial as well as of religious enthusiasm. Pope Clement IV., whose advice he asked, hesitated long before giving his assent, notwithstanding the Holy See's traditional zeal against Islamism. It seems certain that the pious king was not free from generous illusion and confiding credulity in the design and conduct of this crusade, which, in accordance with the interested advice of Charles of Anjou, then king of Sicily, was first directed against Tunis. It may, however, be noted that France now congratulates herself on having planted her flag on the land in which St Louis was the first to display the banner of the *fleurs de lis* together with the oriflamme. Attacked by dysentery, which had declared itself in the army, as he had been attacked before in Egypt, he saw and accepted the approach of death with the feelings which were to be expected from his life and virtues. M. Wallon, summing up the witness of his contemporaries, writes: " His tent became a house of prayer. Mass, and the usual offices of the Church were celebrated there. The cross was raised at the foot of his bed, before his eyes; he kissed it often, and blessing God for all things, he thanked him for his illness. He had with him as confessor Geoffrey of Beaulieu, a close observer of his pious life and virtues, and on this account one of his chief historians. He ministered to the king during his illness, and administered the Communion. One day when the sacred Host was brought to him, St Louis, weak as he was, threw himself out of bed, prostrated himself, and wished to receive it kneeling. It was necessary to carry him back to his bed. When he received extreme unction his voice was scarcely audible, but Queen Margaret's confessor says that it could be seen by the movement of his lips that he took part in the prayers of the rite. Geoffrey of Beaulieu says that he made the responses in the psalms, and that in the litany he himself pronounced the names of the saints and invoked their prayers. Towards the end he was speechless for four days, but always of conscious mind. His eyes were often raised to Heaven, and directed again to those who were with him, on whom he seemed to smile.

"In this extreme weakness, on the day before his death, when Geoffrey of Beaulieu brought him the viaticum, he was resolved to rise to receive it, and kneeling at the foot of the bed with joined hands, he confessed and communicated. The power of speech was therefore not absolutely gone. On the night of his death he was heard to say, 'We shall go to Jerusalem.' It was to the heavenly Jerusalem that his thoughts were thenceforth directed, yet he did not forget the reason of his coming to Africa, and clinging to the end to the vision which had allured his pious soul, he said, ' Let us in God's name seek to have the faith preached in Tunis; who can best fulfil such a mission ? ' and he named a preaching friar who had previously been in that city. When his strength failed and only a low murmur escaped from his lips, he was still invoking the prayers of the saints. Geoffrey of Beaulieu guessed from a few words that he was reciting this end of the prayer of St Denis, 'Lord, grant that for love of Thee we may despise the good things of the world and not fear its evil things'; or it may have been the beginning of the prayer of St James, ' Lord, sanctify and guard Thy people.' Between nine o'clock and noon, after about half an hour's sleep, he opened his eyes, raised them to Heaven with an air of serenity, and spoke the words of the Psalmist: *Introibo in domum tuam, adorabo ad templum sanctum tuum et confitebor nomini tuo.*" At the last moment he had himself laid upon ashes with crossed arms, and rendered up his soul; it was the hour at which our Lord Jesus Christ died upon the cross (August 25, 1270)."

CHAPTER III

THE GOVERNMENT OF ST LOUIS—HIS INTERNAL POLICY

"IT is just," writes William of Nangis, "that we should deplore the death of the good king Louis, by reason of the loss to the whole Church, which he loved so devotedly and which he guarded and defended with all his might. The kingdom of France ought especially to lament his death, to weep and mourn for so good a prince under whom it had peace and joy." We must consider how this good result was produced, what were the guiding principles and characteristic acts of this happy rule by a king who was also a saint.

This is not the place for examining in a general and theoretic way the character, extent and limits of the royal power in St Louis's time. But it can be shown that he exercised it in a full, personal, and, so to say, absolute manner, as it came into his possession and was considered by him to be founded on right and reason. This right appeared to him to be essentially connected with his duty, and hence it was that this prince, who had given such striking proofs of Christian humility, knew how, when occasion arose, to cause his authority to be respected, acting with energy and pride even in the case of his nearest and dearest relations. A knight who had been offended by a judgment given in the local court of Charles of Anjou, appealed to the king, and Charles, in anger, caused him to be put in prison. But the king was told of it. "The pious king," writes Queen Margaret's confessor, "summoned Charles by letters, and when he came before him the king blamed him much, and reproved him for having seized the knight who had appealed, and he said that there could be only one king in France, and it must not be thought because Charles was his brother that any violation of justice could be sanctioned. He caused the prisoner to be released, and when the knight came to pursue his appeal the king himself chose the counsellors and advocates; after long and mature debate the knight was finally pronounced to have gained his cause, and the sentence of the count's court was reversed."

On a still more striking occasion, since justice this time was not involved, we see how St Louis vindicated his royal dignity and slighted authority with imposing rigour. Joinville writes: "Brother Hugh of Jouy, who was marshal of the Temple, was sent to the soldan of Damascus by the Master of the Temple, to make an agreement with the soldan respecting a large tract of land which had been held by the Temple, and which the soldan was willing to divide between the Temple and himself. The convention was made in this sense, subject to the king's consent. And Brother Hugh brought back an emir to represent the soldan, and an authentic copy of the convention.

"The Master told this to the king, at which the king was greatly surprised, and he said that it was very rash to negotiate or conclude a convention with the soldan without first speaking to him about it; and the king required reparation to be made. And the reparation was as follows. The king caused the hangings of three of his pavilions to be raised, and allowed all who wished to come thither from the camp; and there came the Master of the Temple and all his knights, all unshod, across the camp, since their tents were on the outside of it. The king caused the Master of the Temple and the soldan's messenger to be seated before him, and the king said aloud to the Master:

"'Master, you will tell the soldan's messenger that you are grieved to have made a treaty with him without speaking of it to me; and because you have not thus spoken, you release him from all his promises, and render back what he has promised.' The Master took the convention, and delivered it to the emir; and then the Master said, 'I render back the agreement I have wrongly made, and I grieve for my fault.' And then the king told the Master and all his brothers to rise, and thus he spoke: 'Now kneel down and make reparation for what you have done against my will.'

"The Master knelt down, and extended the hem of his mantle to the king, and gave up to the king all their possessions in order that he might decree what reparation was to be made. And the king said, 'First I order that Brother Hugh, who made the convention, shall be banished from the kingdom of

THE KING

Jerusalem.' Nor could the Master, who, together with the king, had stood godfather to the count of Alençon, when he was born at Châtel-Pélcrin, nor could the queen nor any others prevail for Brother Hugh, and he was compelled to leave the Holy Land and the kingdom of Jerusalem."

It has been already shown that St Louis's fervour inclined him to consider that the unction of his consecration invested the kingship with spiritual and almost sacerdotal prerogatives; this was the belief of the Middle Ages, and obtained at all events the tacit assent of the Church. The distinction—we do not say the separation, which must always be deplored—between the spiritual and temporal orders was at that time much less clearly understood and defined than has since been the case in the teaching of theology, philosophy and politics, yet this distinction subsisted in its chief lines, derived from the Gospel and from Catholic tradition, in the minds of the learned and thoughtful clergy. William of Chartres, who had become a Dominican religious, makes use of the curious expression, "*pia usurpatio*," in speaking of St Louis's zeal for the apostolate, which was not merely personal, but royal, and the praise seems to be accompanied by a slight reservation of theoretic right. An analogous feeling was perhaps apparent in the prudent advice given by Clement IV. to the pious king, desiring him to moderate his wrath against the use, too common then and since, of blasphemous oaths; advice given with that admirable and excellent moderation which is the characteristic feature of the Holy See, save in essential cases and circumstances of imperious urgency.[1]

St Louis held this vice in special abhorrence. He taught his son Philip that "no reviling of God and His saints should be suffered in his presence without speedy punishment." And he adds a little later, "Be very diligent in uprooting sins from the land, such as wicked oaths, and all which is done or said in contempt of God, of our Lady, and of the saints." He proposed to proclaim severer penalties for blasphemy in his kingdom, but his zeal was justly considered excessive in Rome, and the Pope sought to moderate it. M. Wallon writes: "In a Bull of the 12th July 1268, Clement IV. commends the pious king for his zeal, but exhorts him to moderate it; and if he recalls the punishments awarded in the Old Testament, it is to persuade him not to follow the precedent, and to punish without injury to the limbs or life of the guilty. The advice is repeated in a letter of the same date, addressed to the barons of France, with whom he knew that the king liked to take counsel. The warning was obeyed. The decree of 1269 prescribed a fine; the pillory and imprisonment for those who could not pay it, and a whipping for children from ten to fourteen years of age. The king, however, reserved the rights of punishing with greater severity any more monstrous blasphemies which might be reported to him."

---

[1] This hypothesis must not, however, be pressed too far, since it is certain that even in the text in which he opposes excessive rigour, he distinctly approves of the repression of blasphemy by the civil power and by means of temporal punishment.

In some special cases the king, in fact, gave free course to his anger. Joinville mentions two instances in which St Louis, although it is probable that he did not himself make the distinction, seems to have acted less with respect to the legislative and administrative power of a king, strictly so-called, than in virtue of the patriarchal and arbitrary authority, which, according to ancient usage, not yet altogether fallen into disuse, pertained to the great lords over the common people, formerly serfs, born or dwelling on their lands: "The king loved God and His sweet Mother so well, that all those convicted of speaking dishonourably of God or His Mother, or of some vile oath, were grievously punished by him. Thus I saw him place a goldsmith on a ladder at Cæserea, in shirt and drawers, with a pig's entrails round his neck, in such abundance that they reached his nose. I have heard that after I returned from Cæserea he caused the lip and nose of a citizen of Paris to be burnt with a hot iron kept for this purpose, but this I did not see. And, in reply to the murmurs caused by this punishment, the holy king said, 'I would myself be branded with a hot iron, if thereby my kingdom might be delivered from all vile oaths.'"

Regal power, not infinite, but at that time indefinite, was united in St Louis's person with seignorial and patriarchal authority, and this made him in his own domains a prince who could exact absolute obedience; the prestige of his crown and virtues, combined with the ascendancy achieved by Philip Augustus, maintained by Louis VIII., defended and increased by Blanche of Castile, caused him to be throughout the kingdom a suzerain and a feared and respected sovereign. But his sensitive conscience and his naturally thoughtful and deliberative turn of mind inspired him with one of the best traditions of his ancestors, which he transmitted in a still more marked degree to his descendants, that of coming to a decision in council after mature examination. The eminently *consultative* character of the Capet monarchy, so marked even in Louis XIV., is one of the characteristic features of St Louis's rule, although, as M. de Wailly has noted, this did not prevent the king, under certain circumstances, when his mind was clearly made up, from allowing his judgment to outweigh the contrary advice of his counsellors. In the case of legislative acts applicable to the whole kingdom, he could not, however, dispense with the formal assent of the great feudatories, who enjoyed a species of sovereignty in their own domains, and were in many respects independent. But his moral authority and example had great power over them and their subjects, who, notwithstanding their intermediate rulers, were, after all, proud of being also subjects of the king.

Justice was the leading principle of St Louis's rule, as it was the dominant quality of his moral character. "Dear son," he writes in his *Instructions*, "if you come to reign, do that which befits a king, that is, be so just as to deviate in nothing from justice, whatever may befall you. If a poor man goes to law with one who is rich, support the poor rather than the rich man until you know the truth, and when the truth is known, do that which is just. . . . And if it

THE KING

happen that any man has a dispute with yourself, maintain the cause of your adversary before the council, so as not to appear partial to your own cause, until the truth is known. Unless you do this, those who are of the council may fear to speak against you, and this ought not to be. . . . And if you find that you possess anything unjustly acquired, either in your time or in that of your predecessors, make restitution at once, however great its value, either in land, money, or any other thing. . . . If the matter is doubtful and you cannot find out the truth, follow the advice of trusty men, and make such an agreement as may fully deliver your soul and that of your predecessors. If you hear that your predecessors have made restitution of anything, take great trouble to discover if anything more should be restored, and if you find that this is the case, restore it at once so as to deliver your own soul and that of your predecessors."

He gave a splendid and unprecedented proof of his adherence to these noble maxims in the great inquiry ordained by him in 1247, before his approaching departure for the Crusade. M. Elie Berger writes: "As he wished to be in a state of grace at the moment of departure, and to take with him to the Holy Land a quiet conscience by leaving the kingdom in as happy condition as possible, he resolved to carry out one of the noblest measures ever undertaken by a king. By his order, inquisitors were sent into all the provinces annexed to the royal dominion since the accession of Philip Augustus. All those who had been maltreated or despoiled by the bailiffs, seneschals, provosts, sergeants, and other representatives of the royal authority, came to declare their wrongs to these newly appointed judges, and to demand the reparation which was due to them; the number was great, since for forty years there had been much suffering in the country districts and even in the towns. . . . The royal officers had too often acted as if they were in a conquered country; they believed themselves to be safe from observation, so that they might do as they pleased. The people had much to endure during these forty years, and it was a noble idea to make reparation freely and with elaborate care. No prince had been known, of his own accord and at his own cost, to redress the wrongs inflicted on the people during the reigns of his father and grandfather. This made an immense impression, which lasted for centuries. Blanche's son was not merely a good king, he became the unrivalled sovereign, the impeccable judge, the friend and consoler of his subjects."

A king so little disposed to spare himself when justice was in question was as little likely to give way to others. We have already heard of his advice to his son: "Take heed lest your love for any person should cause you to deviate from justice." We have seen that he applied this rule to his own brother, and Queen Margaret's confessor reports another instance, also concerning the same Charles of Anjou, "Once, when the pious king was in Paris, several citizens and merchants complained to him that his brother Charles, to whom they had lent money and sold merchandise, would not satisfy their claims. The king then ordered Monseigneur Charles to pay them. And because Monseigneur Charles declined to pay them and was disposed to contest the matter, the king said that if he did not pay he would be deprived of the estates held by him, and it was believed that Monseigneur Charles satisfied their claims by order of the pious king."

Another counsel in the *Instructions* is prompted by the same principle: "Dear son, be careful to have good bailiffs and good provosts on your lands, and make frequent inquiry whether their judgments are just, and whether they do wrong to any man." M. Lecoy de la Marche gives a summary of his great decree of 1254 for the reformation of the kingdom, which anticipates this advice.

"Under penalty of chastisement by the king, the seneschals and other royal officers shall take and observe an oath to render justice without respect of persons, in accordance with the approved customs and usages; to maintain the rights of the sovereign without prejudice to those of individuals; to receive no present for themselves, their wives and children, and to return any they may have received; never to borrow from those subject to them more than a small sum, below twenty livres, and to repay this within two months; to take no share in the profit of sales, or in appointments to subordinate offices, or in rents due to the king, or in coinage or the like; not to protect subaltern officers who have been guilty of malversation or of abuse of power, or who are suspected of usury or of leading a scandalous life, but on the contrary to correct them. . . . They shall buy no property in their district without the king's leave, on pain of confiscation. They shall not take a wife for themselves, their relations or their servants. They shall not cause their relations and servants to be received into monasteries, nor shall they procure for them ecclesiastical benefices. They shall not eat nor sleep in the religious houses without the king's leave. They shall only have a small number of beadles or of sergeants to carry out their sentences; these sergeants must be publicly nominated at the assizes, and are only to be obeyed when provided with a regular mandate from their superior. The seneschals, bailiffs and their subordinates shall arrest no one for debt, unless it be for sums due to the king. They shall not detain a person accused of crime if he is in a condition to purge himself of the accusation, unless the crime is very great, or if he is convicted on his own confession, or by very strong proofs or presumptions. The inquiry drawn up against the accused shall be communicated to him. Persons of good fame, even the poor, shall not be put to the question on the testimony of a single witness. Those who have bought inferior offices may not sell them again, and if there are many buyers one only shall administer justice. The seneschals and bailiffs shall hold audience in the accustomed places. They shall not charge the people with any imposition. They shall not impress horses save for necessary causes, and they may not exact money from those who are willing to serve in person. They shall only forbid the exportation of wine, wheat, and other goods, after a deliberation in council. . . . When their functions are ended the royal officers shall remain in the place for fifty days, so as to reply to any complaints of which they may be the object."

However desirous the holy king might be for the rule of justice and the reformation of abuses, he was powerless in some cases, because he had to do with the hitherto unavoidable necessities of feudal administration. Such was the putting up to auction of offices and inferior magistracies and provostships. During St Louis's minority this abuse extended to the administration of the capital itself, which was regulated, without the authority of the king, by a viscount chosen from among the chief seigneurs of the kingdom. In this case the matter was serious, and the royal hand intervened. Joinville writes: "The provostship of Paris was at that time sold to the citizens of Paris or to some others, and those who bought it protected their children and nephews in their misdeeds; for those young men relied on their relations and friends who held the provostship. For this cause the poor were trampled under foot and could get no justice from the rich, who gave great presents and gifts to the provosts.

" He who at that time spoke the truth before the provosts, or who wished to keep his oath, so as not to be perjured, with respect to a debt or anything else with which he was charged, was fined and punished by the provost. On account of the great injustice and robbery committed in the provostship, the poor did not dare to remain on the king's domain, but went to dwell in other seignories.

And the king's domain was so forsaken, that when the provost held his pleadings, only ten or twelve persons came.

"Besides this, there were so many criminals and thieves in Paris and the neighbourhood that the country was full of them. The king, who was very careful to protect the poor, knew all the truth; then he would no longer allow the provostship of Paris to be sold, but he gave great and good wages to those who thenceforward held it. And he put an end to all the grievous impositions with which the people was burdened, and he caused inquiry to be made in all the kingdom and throughout the country for a man who would do worthy and strict justice, and who would spare the rich man no more than the poor.

"Stephen Boileau was then suggested to him, and he fulfilled the office of provost so well that no malefactor nor thief nor murderer dared to remain in Paris who was not at once hanged or otherwise put to death; neither his relations nor his descent, nor gold nor silver, could save him. The king's domain began to amend, and people came to live there because justice was done. It was so much amended and so much more thickly peopled, that the money received by the king from sales, purchases, seizures, and other things, was double what it had been before."

In order to effect a more general oversight by the central power, which was rendered necessary by the conditions of administration at that time, St Louis, struck with the result of the inquiry in 1247, estab-

THE KING

lished the habitual practice of these reviews and administrative inspections as a regular institution of his government. The royal inquisitors, charged to ascertain, to repress and to correct abuses and injustice, were generally chosen by him from members of the regular clergy, and especially from the two great orders recently established of St Francis and St Dominic; these orders were dear to the pious king, and really offered to him higher guarantees of disinterestedness and elevation of mind. It is to this thirst for justice that we must refer the personal share which he took in the persevering and tenacious assumption of regal rights, asserted by the members of the house of Capet to remedy the evils of feudal sub-division; appeals and cases for the king's decision were multiplied and regulated, and the organisation of the supreme court was more precisely defined; that is, of the royal council considered in its judiciary functions, to which was given in France the name of parliament. This term, at first applied in a special sense and subsequently exclusively to judicial functions, was in St Louis's time generally applied to all assemblies of seigneurs and prelates summoned by the king to deliberate on any important business.

In the conception of the kingship, as it existed in the Middle Ages, the quality of sovereign judge was inherent in the person of the monarch, and when he delegated this essential part of his rights and duty to magistrates appointed by him, he by no means renounced the right of exercising it in person when it seemed good to him. St Louis took pleasure in such exercise, to which was added that of the patriarchal authority of which we have spoken above. Joinville has shown him to us under this aspect in a celebrated passage, one of those historic pictures which live in the memory of all:

"The king so arranged matters that Monseigneur de Nesle and the good count of Soissons, and we others who were with him, when we had heard mass, should go to hear the pleadings of the gate, now called the requests.

"And when he came out of church, he sent for us, and sat down at the foot of the bed, and caused us to be seated round him, and he asked if there were any pleaders to dismiss who could not be dismissed without him. And we gave their names, and he ordered them to be fetched, and he asked of them, 'Why do you not take that which your people offer?' And they said, 'Sire, it is because they offer little.' And he spake thus, 'You ought to take what they are willing to offer.' And the holy man endeavoured thus with all his might to set them in the right and reasonable way.

"It often happened in summer that he went after mass to sit in the wood of Vincennes, and leaned his back against an oak tree, and bade us sit round him. And all those who had business came to speak to him, not hindered by his guards nor by other people. And then he would ask with his own mouth: 'Is any one here who has a cause?' And those who had a cause stood up. And then he said: 'Be silent all of you, that we may take one after the other.' And then he would call Monseigneur Peter of Fontaines and Monseigneur Geoffrey of Villette, and would say to one of them: 'Decide this cause for me.'

"And when he found anything to correct in the words of those who spoke for him, or in the words of those who spoke for others, he himself spoke the correction with his own mouth. Sometimes in summer I have seen him come into his garden in Paris to decide causes, wearing a camlet tunic, a sur-coat without sleeves, a mantle of black taffety round his neck, his hair well combed and flowing, a cap made of the feathers of a white peacock on his head. And he would have carpets spread that we might sit round him, and all the people who brought causes before him stood up in his presence. And then he would dismiss them after the manner of which I have told you in the wood of Vincennes."

This firm love of justice which St Louis expressed in the maxim: "To every man his right," naturally inspired his mind and administration with the taste for order and reason which may be expressed in the formula: "Everything in its right place." Although he had a profound respect for tradition, he did not hesitate to violate it when his conscience, enlightened by christian faith, showed it to be opposed to moral truth. It was thus that he absolutely proscribed through his dominions the absurd and cruel practice of the judicial duel, although the custom had endured for ages, transported from the forests of Germany into Gaul, and had struck deep root in feudal institutions and customs. "We forbid such combats throughout our dominions," he said peremptorily in the first article of his celebrated ordinance of 1260, "and we substitute the testimony of witnesses for these combats." M. Lecoy de la Marche writes that: "even in the crown domains the nobles offered a strong opposition." The prejudice was so strong that the duel in criminal causes was re-established under Philip the Fair, and it was continued, although more and more restricted in its application and dissimulated under different forms, up to the time of the famous combat between La Chataigneraic and Jarnac, which took place in 1547 in the presence of the court. It was then only that Jarnac's fatal blow led to the absolute interdiction of such encounters. Unhappily, as we know too well, in spite of Richelieu's severe edicts, maintained and confirmed by Louis XIV., the private duel, the offspring of the judicial duel, has been continued to this day, to the great prejudice and sometimes to the great scandal of reason and equity.

When order is applied to the management of finance it is called economy, and economy is not merely a private, but, in the highest degree, a kingly virtue. Such at least was St Louis's opinion. "Dear son," he writes in his *Instructions*, "I exhort you to take great care that the money you expend may be well spent and justly acquired. And I greatly desire this quality for you, that you may refrain from foolish expenditure and from grievous exactions, and that your money may be well placed and well taken." Owing to this mode, in all times too much forgotten, of managing his affairs, of receiving and of spending his treasure, St Louis was able to meet the enormous expenses of the crusades, as well as of his lavish endowments and almsgiving, without oppressing his people. Joinville writes: "In this expedition (the war of Poitou and Saintonge) the king gave great gifts, as I have heard from those who took part in it. But neither for these gifts, nor for the expenses of the expedition, nor in others beyond seas and at home, did the king ever demand or take help which caused his barons and his good towns to make complaint."

The high standard of his coinage, of which the tradition remained in later years, is a technical detail of St Louis's reign, and perhaps not the least significant fact which attests his royal virtues. M. Faure writes: "It was in St Louis's reign that the fine types of gold and silver coins were produced, which are no less remarkable for their purity of metal than for the elegance of their impressions, so much admired by antiquaries. Their high value tempted the succeeding kings, who debased the coinage. The changes made by his grandson, Philip the Fair, shook the confidence of the people in the royal coinage. The State collected the taxes in good money, and put it back into circulation under the same denominations in coins of inferior value. In this manner the people paid twice over to their ruin, and they demanded with outcries that St Louis's coinage should be given back to them."

Together with his love of justice, St Louis's love of peace is the feature of his royal character which his contemporaries thought most remarkable: "*rex ipse pacificus*," according to the expression of William of Chartres, cited above. This disposition, which cannot be too highly honoured in the leaders of men, is displayed in touching terms in his *Instructions* to his son Philip: "Dear son, I exhort you to apply yourself diligently, according as you are able, to put an end to wars and disputes on your own domain and those of your followers, since this is a thing very pleasing to our Lord. And of this St Martin has given a great example. For when he knew by a warning from our Lord that he was about to die, he set about making peace between certain clerks in his archbishopric, and it seemed to him that in so doing he should end his life worthily." The same thing is expressed with brevity and admirable force in the preamble to the ordinance of reformation of 1254: "As the kingly power is bound to do, we desire the peace and repose of our subjects most heartily, a repose in which we ourselves shall find rest." His desire for peace entitled him to Pope Urban IV.'s noble praise: "You whom Divine power has set in your kingdom as an angel of peace, and who, possessing the gifts of a pacific king can destroy the roots of discord and sow the seeds of peace. You, not abusing the greatness of your power, but ruling your subjects with mercy and kindness, constantly endeavour that they should enjoy the peace desired of all men and taste the benefits of a life free from tumult and fear."

To this profound and thoughtful passion for general peace we must refer St Louis's efforts to deliver France from the terrible Germanic and feudal custom of waging private wars; a custom which the Church herself had only been able, in the eleventh and twelth centuries, to moderate by the Peace and Truce of God. The *quarantaine du roi*, devised and imposed, as it is said, by Philip Augustus, in order to prevent hostilities between the barons, was energetically renewed and confirmed by St Louis. But he afterwards went further and absolutely prohibited private wars among the nobles in his dominion. "You must know," he said in a decree of 1257, " that by the advice of our council we have prohibited in our kingdom all wars, the burning of houses and the laying waste of tilled lands. Therefore, by precise and special order, we command you to abstain, in conformity with the said prohibition, from war or arson, and from interference with the work of labourers. For if you presume to infringe this edict, we order our seneschal to give aid with zeal and devotion to our beloved and trusty Guy, Bishop elect of Puy (subsequently Clement IV.), to maintain peace in his diocese, and to punish peace-breakers according to the exigency of the case."

Justice and peace were indeed a great benefit and great advance at this time of transition from the heroic, yet terrible whirlwind of early feudal times. But St Louis was inspired by a christian beneficence to make more direct efforts for his people. He gave solace, at once material and moral, to the miseries of that time, and the radiation of his sympathy and alms extended far beyond his presence and his immediate circle. Queen Margaret's confessor writes: "When the king learned that there was great scarcity of food in any part of his dominions, he sent by his sergeants 3000 or sometimes 5000 *livres tournois*, according to the need.[1] The scarcity was at one time so great that the king sent a sum of money to Normandy for the poor, and he ordered those in charge of it to take special care for the poor directly dependent on the king and who paid an annual rent to him, in case they were more needy than others." We owe to the same biographer this charming and instructive anecdote: "Once when the king was passing through the town of Chateauneuf-sur-Loire, at the entry to the town, outside the castle, a poor aged woman, who stood at the door of her cottage, with a morsel of bread in her hand, said to the pious king: 'Good king, my husband, who lies here sick, is nourished with this bread which is your gift'; and the king took the bread in his hand and said: 'This is rather bitter bread,' and when the pious king heard that the sick man was in the cottage, he went in thither to visit him."

More enduring help, since it extended from the present to the future, was afforded by his numerous religious foundations, especially refuges and hospitals. "The pious king," writes the confessor, "caused a piece of ground near St Honoré to be bought, and a large house to be built on it, in order that three hundred of the indigent blind might always inhabit it; and they had an annual pension from the king's purse for vegetables and other things. And a church, which he dedicated to St Remi, is attached to the house, in which the said blind can hear divine service.

[1] M. de Wailly estimates the value of the *livre tournois* at about fifteen shillings, that of the *livre parisis* at about eighteen shillings. But we have not only to consider the intrinsic value. Money was of a much higher purchasing power than it is now.

THE KING

And it often happened that on the feast day of St Remi, on which day the office was solemnly chanted by the blind, the pious king came to the church where the blind were assembled around him, and he supported this church. Moreover, he founded and built the hospital of Vernon, and as it is placed in the best part of the town, and occupies a large space, the pious king did not spend less than 30,000 *livres parisis* on the land and the buildings. . . . Again he caused the hospital of Pontoise to be built; he founded and endowed it with possessions which brought in an annual income of four hundred livres. And again he established the hospital of Compiègne and enlarged it at great cost; on this work he expended 12,000 *livres parisis*. . . . Again, he enlarged the hospital of Paris, which was extended to the *Petit-Pont*, and endowed it with money." M. Faure relates a touching anecdote with respect this celebrated house, " There was in one year a lack of wine for the sick in the Paris hospital, and it was embarrassed in other ways. The director, who was at that time called the master, at a loss what to do, went to implore the king's help. A hundred livres would have put him at his ease, and since he knew the king's generosity, he hoped to obtain it. But he had scarcely set forth the distress of his poor patients, than the king turned to his almoner and ordered him to give a thousand livres. The master thought that he had not heard aright, and the king repeated : ' Give a thousand livres for the poor of the Paris hospital.' "

We have already had occasion to note what may

be called St Louis's intellectual charity in founding the library of the Sainte Chapelle. We have another proof of this in the effectual aid he gave to Robert of Sorbon in the foundation of the college which afterwards became the Sorbonne. "Of this," says Tillemont, "St Louis was in part the founder. . . . I do not know whether we are to refer to this what we are told of St Louis's purchase of two streets of houses before the palace of Thermes, in order to erect large buildings for the housing of poor students, who were to be received by those authorised to receive them, and the other buildings were let for the benefit of these poor students and of others. This cost the king at least 4000 *livres tournois*." The royal and personal solicitude shown by St Louis for the poor students is attested by Margaret's confessor: " The holy king made an allowance out of his treasury every week to poor clerks, so as to enable them to frequent the schools, and it is believed that the number of poor scholars thus aided by the king was at least a hundred." We do not think it an anachronism to ascribe to this wise and holy king, as one of the qualities of his mind and soul, a desire of progress, too often carried to excess in our day, but prudently exercised by him. He has indeed done more, for he uttered this distinct advice in his *Instructions* to his heir: " Be in all things the promoter of good, according as you are able."

Justice, order and reason, peace, love of that which is good and desire of that which is better; such were the guiding principles of St Louis' rule. We must now look more closely into the mode, relying on these principles, in which he understood and practised the relations of his rule with the different parties which constituted the French society of that day.

As mother of this society, for she may really claim such a title, the Catholic Church and her two orders of clergy took a very prominent place. Her religious rights, recognised and guaranteed by the civil power, had become social rights, and since at the same time she was, by reason of her territorial possessions, herself included in the organisation of the feudal hierarchy, this double claim, social and feudal, had acquired for her the legitimate exercise of numerous temporal rights and privileges. The keeping and direction of these several rights pertained to her chiefs, the bishops or abbots, and to the supreme chief of the Church, to the sovereign Pontiff. It followed from this state of things, even in the domain of politics and justice, that there was a perpetual contact and, as it were, an interlacing of the two societies, lay and clerical, which constituted only one nation, and this perpetual contact and interlacing led, owing to the weakness of human nature, to frequent conflicts, as well as to many good results. It has been much disputed what was the attitude of St Louis in these constant relations and occasional conflicts, even since learned men have agreed to reject as unauthentic the celebrated pragmatic sanction, from which much information was derived, now shown to be valueless. We may leave the discussion of particular facts to authors whose labours claim examination and appreciation, and apply ourselves to those features which are essential, or at any rate characteristic.

St Louis's general disposition is not doubtful, since it is expressly declared in the unimpeachable text of his *Instructions*. " Be very diligent to watch over all sorts of people in the kingdom, and especially over the persons of Holy Church, and defend them from all violence done to their persons or goods. And I wish you to remember the words of my predecessor, King Philip, which were heard and repeated to me by a member of his council. The king was once with his privy council, at which he who repeated his words to me was present. And those of his council told him of many wrongs done by the clergy, and that many people wondered how he could suffer it. And he answered: ' I know that they have wronged me in many things, but when I remember how our Lord has honoured me, I would rather suffer injury than do anything to bring discord between me and Holy Church.' And I tell you this, so that you may not lightly believe in the wrongs alleged against the persons of Holy Church, but rather honour them and watch over them, so that they may fulfil the service of our Lord in peace. I also enjoin you to show special affection to the religious, and to succour them in their needs; and love more than others those by whom you believe that our Lord is more honoured and better served. . . . Dear son, I enjoin you to be always devoted to the Roman Church and to the sovereign Pontiff, our father, and to render to him the honour and reverence which you owe to him, your spiritual father."

THE KING

St Louis's spirit in the relations of his government to the Church and her chief is therefore quite clear, and it is a spirit of cordial understanding, even at the cost of concessions on his part. Yet it must not be said that he always thought it right to give way, for certain texts prove the contrary. In several cases he maintained in word and act that which he regarded as his right, and he supported, at any rate provisionally, the acts of his agents. The sovereign Pontiffs sometimes complained to him of his councillors and officers, more rarely of himself, and always with special courtesy. The harmony between him and the Holy See was on the whole constant and exemplary. With respect to his excellent relations with Clement IV., the Bollandists, as M. Lecoy de la Marche observes, have rather happily defined their reciprocal situation: "The one refused to the other that which he did feel himself justified in conceding, and their friendship did not suffer from it." M. Elie Berger writes, in speaking of some difficulties between St Louis and Innocent IV.: "that the relations between these two persons, who had so much reason for remaining united, continued to be correct and friendly." This is to say too little; they were affectionate on both sides, and should rather be termed paternal and filial.

The pious king had some rather lively disputes with the higher clergy of France, notwithstanding their habitual agreement. It has pleased Joinville to enlarge on this subject. We must undoubtedly take account of his narrative, while taking care not to forget that the sentiments of the seneschal of

Champagne were very seigniorial, and therefore by no means impartial, as we shall see in his proceedings against the abbey of St Urban, which can hardly be justified. We must hear what he has to say, but not without reserve, at any rate as far as concerns his tone, for it would not be in conformity with a healthy criticism to accept him in this instance as an altogether trustworthy interpreter of his saintly friend's sentiments, since we are able to draw from a much more direct source, of which the authority is unequalled.

"I must," Joinville writes, "tell you of his wisdom. On one occasion it was declared that there was no one on his council so wise as he was. And this was shown when men spoke to him on certain matters, since he did not say, 'I will take council,' but when he saw the right course to be clear and evident, he answered alone and at once, without taking counsel; thus I have heard that he replied to all the prelates of the kingdom of France on a request made to him, which was as follows:

"The bishop Guy of Auxerre spoke to him for the rest. 'Sire,' said he, 'the archbishops who are here have charged me to tell you that Christianity languishes and perishes in your hands, and that if you do not take care it will languish still more, because no one now fears an excommunication. We therefore, sire, require you to give orders to your bailiffs and sergeants to constrain the excommunicate who have been under sentence for a year and a day to make satisfaction to the Church.' And the king answered alone, without taking counsel, that he would, as they required, willingly give orders to his bailiffs and sergeants to put force on the excommunicate, provided he was made acquainted with the sentence, so as to judge whether it were just or not.

"And they consulted together, and answered the king that they could not acquaint him with that which pertained to the ecclesiastical tribunal. And the king answered in his turn that he could not acquaint them with that which pertained to himself, and that he would not order his sergeants to constrain the excommunicate to ask for absolution, whether it were just or unjust. 'For if I did this, I should act against God and against justice. And of this I give you an instance, since the bishops of Brittany held the count of Brittany under excommunication for seven years, after which he was absolved by the Court of Rome; and if I had put force upon him in the first year, I should have done amiss.'[1]

"It happened, after our return from over sea, that the monks of St Urban elected two abbots; Peter, bishop of Châlons, whom may God forgive, dismissed them both, and consecrated John of Mymeri as abbot, and gave him the crozier.[2] I would not accept him as abbot, since he had wronged the abbot Geoffrey, who had appealed against him and gone to

[1] The argument here used by St Louis must be specially noted. We know, in fact, that the Holy See recognised the mode in which excommunications were then abused, and that Gregory IV. and Innocent IV. were busied in finding a remedy for it.

[2] We have here the seneschal's story, but there is, as we have already noted, another, not altogether to Joinville's honour, of which we are informed by François Delaborde and Gaston Paris.

Rome. I kept the abbey in my own hands until the said Geoffrey obtained the crozier, and it was lost by the monk to whom the bishop had given it, and the bishop excommunicated me while the dispute lasted. A parliament was therefore held at Paris, at which there was a great contest between me and the bishop Peter of Châlons, and between countess Margaret of Flanders and the archbishop of Rheims, whom she denounced.

"At the next parliament all the prelates implored the king to come and speak to them alone. When he returned from speaking to them, he came to us who waited for him in the pleading chamber, and told us with a smile of the trouble he had had with the prelates; the first was that the archbishop of Rheims said to the king, 'Sire, what amends will you make for taking from me the charge of St Remi of Rheims? For by those very relics, I would not for all the kingdom of France have such a sin upon my conscience.' 'By those relics,' said the king, 'I declare that you would do as much for Compiègne alone, so great is your covetousness. And now one of us two has perjured himself.

"'The bishop of Chartres demanded of me,' said the king, 'that I should give up to him that which was his. And I told him that I should not do so until he had paid what was due to me. And I told him that he had done homage to me with his hand in mine, and that when he sought to disinherit me he did not act well and loyally.'

"'The bishop of Châlons asked of me,' said the king, 'Sire, what will you do to the seigneur of

Joinville, who has deprived this poor monk of the abbey of St Urban?' 'My lord bishop,' said the king, 'you have ordained among yourselves that no excommunicate person is to be heard in the lay courts, and I have seen that you are excommunicated by a letter sealed with thirty-two seals; wherefore I shall not hear you until you have obtained absolution.' And I tell you these things in order that you may see clearly how he all alone was able by his good sense to deal with what he had to do.

"The abbot Geoffrey of St Urban, after all that I had done for him, returned evil for good, and appealed against me. He let our holy king know that he maintained his rights. I asked the king to make known the truth on this point, whether the right was on his side or mine. 'Sire,' said the abbot, 'may it please God that you should not do this, but rather order the cause to be pleaded between me and the lord of Joinville, for we would sooner have the abbey in your keeping than in that of the man whose heritage it is.' Then the king said to me, 'Do they speak truly in saying that the abbey is in my keeping?' 'Certainly, sire,' I said, 'it is not so, but it is mine.'

"Then the king said, 'It may well be that the heritage is yours, but that you have no right to keep this abbey. But he said to the abbot, 'according to what you say, and to what the seneschal says, it is necessary that the abbey should remain with me, or with him. I shall not cease to make the truth known, whatever you may say, for if I should compel him to plead I should do wrong to him who is my own servant, in thus causing him to plead for his rights when he has offered to make those rights clearly known to me.' He therefore sought out the truth, and when the truth was known he delivered the keeping of the abbey to me, and made over its deeds to me."

This intimate connection between the temporal and spiritual powers continued, in spite of some differences of detail, to be the social and political law of St Louis's time; and while the ecclesiastical power exercised numerous temporal rights, the civil power was, on the other hand, as it is to this day, invested by the consent of the Church with certain rights which have to do with the spiritual authority. Such was the collation to a great number of benefices, involving the nomination by the king of titulars to ecclesiastical functions, and to the revenues pertaining to these benefices. It is scarcely necessary to note the sentiments by which St Louis was inspired in the exercise of such a right. Here is his advice to his son Philip on this point: " Dear son, I enjoin you to give the benefices of Holy Church which you have to give away to virtuous persons, after taking careful counsel with discreet men. And it is in my opinion better to give them to those who have not yet received a prebend, than to others. For, if you make sufficient inquiry, you will find clerks enough who have nothing, and who are fit to hold these benefices."

In St Louis's day the nobles, who were in feudal times above all things a military and territorial aristocracy, constituted a social and political force of the first importance, and one of the fundamental institutions of the country. But their power, which had formerly been excessive, was declining, owing to the repeated shocks it had received since the time of Louis VI., from the Capet dynasty. In this respect Louis IX. followed on the whole the anti-feudal policy of his predecessors, since he considered it to be in conformity with reason, public order, and his own exalted idea of the duty of a king, but he acted within the limits of a scrupulous equity, and permitted himself, even for good ends, no violation of clearly established rights. Of this Queen Margaret's confessor gives a curious instance. "In the churchyard of the parish church of Vitry the pious king once heard a sermon by Friar Lambert, in the presence of a great multitude of people. Now it happened that there was a tavern somewhat near to the said churchyard, in which a number of men had assembled who made a great noise, so that they disturbed the preacher and his hearers. The king then asked in whose jurisdiction this place was, and he was told that it pertained to himself; and then he ordered some of his sergeants to put to silence these people who disturbed God's word; which was done. And it is supposed that the king inquired to whom the jurisdiction belonged in order that if it was not his own he might not interfere with the jurisdiction and seignory of others."

But his hereditary tendency, as well as his evident love of justice, is clearly shown in the almost inflexible rigour of his severity towards faults committed by the chief nobles. The case of Enguerrard de Coucy, one of the first barons of the kingdom, chief of one of the most illustrious and powerful houses, next to those of the great feudatories, has become justly famous. We take the story from M. Wallon, who has summed up the confessor's rather diffuse narrative with his usual clearness.

"Three young nobles of the county of Flanders were suprised, together with the abbot of St Nicholas, in a wood pertaining to Coucy, with bows and arrows. Although they had neither dogs nor hunting implements, they were found guilty of having gone out to hunt, and were hanged. The abbot and several women of their families made complaint to the king, and Enguerrard was arrested and taken to the Louvre.[1] The king summoned him before him; he appeared, having with him the king of Navarre, the king of Burgundy, the counts of Bar, Soissons, Brittany, and Blois, the archbishop of Rheims, sire John of Thorote, and nearly all the great men in the kingdom. The accused said that he wished to take counsel, and he retired with most of the seigneurs who had accompanied him, leaving the king alone with his household. When he returned, John of Thorote, in his name, said that he would not submit to this inquiry, since his person, his honour, and his heritage were at stake, but that he was ready to do battle, denying that he had hanged the three young men, or ordered them to be hanged. His only opponents were the abbot and the women, who

[1] The Louvre was at that time a fortress and prison. The king's palace was in the *Cité*.

were there to ask for justice. The king answered that in causes in which the poor, the churches, and persons worthy of pity, took part, it was not fitting to decide them in battle; for it was not easy to find anyone to fight for such sorts of people against the barons of the kingdom. He said that his action against the accused was no new thing, and he alleged the example of his predecessor Philip Augustus. He therefore agreed to the request of the complainants, and caused Enguerrard to be arrested by the sergeants and taken to the Louvre. All prayers were useless; St Louis refused to hear them, rose from his seat, and the barons went away astonished and confused.

"They did not, however, consider that they were beaten. They again came together; the king of Navarre, the count of Brittany, and with them the countess of Flanders, who ought rather to have intervened for the victims. It was as if they had conspired against the king's power and honour; for they were not content to implore Coucy's release, but asserted that he could not be kept in prison. The count of Brittany maintained that the king had no right to institute inquiries against the barons of his kingdom in matters which concerned their persons, their heritage or their honour. The king replied, 'You did not speak thus in former times when the barons in direct dependence upon you came before me with complaints against yourself, and offered to sustain them in battle. You then said that to do battle was not in the way of justice.' The barons put forward a final argument, namely, that according to the customs of the kingdom, the king could only judge the accused and punish him in person after an inquiry to which he had refused to submit. The king was resolute, and declared that neither the rank of the guilty man nor the power of his friends should prevent him from doing full justice. Coucy's life was, however, spared. The fact that he had not been present at the judgment, nor at the execution, prevailed in his favour. By the advice of his counsellors the king condemned him to pay 1200 *livres parisis*, which, considering the difference in the purchasing power of money, may be estimated at considerably more than £400,000, and he sent this sum to St John of Acre for the defence of Palestine. The wood in which the young men were hanged was confiscated to the abbey of St Nicholas. The condemned man was also constrained to found three perpetual chapelries for the souls of his victims, and he forfeited jurisdiction over his woods and fish ponds, so that he was forbidden to imprison or execute for any offence which had to do with them. Since Enguerrard's defender, John of Thorote, had in his anger told the barons that the king would do well to hang them all, the king, who had been told of this, sent for him and said, 'How comes it, John, that you have said I should hang my barons? I certainly will not have them hanged, but I will punish them when they do amiss.' John of Thorote denied that he had said this, and offered to justify himself on the oath of twenty or thirty knights. The king would not carry the matter further, and let him go."

This noteworthy instance does not stand alone.

An unfaithful wife, belonging to one of the most considerable families in Pontoise, had procured the death of her husband by her accomplice, and threw the corpse into a privy. When brought to trial she confessed her crime, and expressed her deep repentance. The queen herself, with the countess of Poitiers and other great ladies, implored the king to remit the sentence of death. The king refused. The prayers of several religious, preaching and minor friars, who were touched by the sentiments expressed by the guilty woman, were equally unavailing. But the queen and others implored him that at any rate, out of consideration for the family, the execution should not take place at Pontoise. "And then," as we are told by Margaret's confessor, "the king asked the advice of a noble and wise man, Simon of Nesle, and Simon replied that justice ought to be publickly done. Then the pious king ordered the said woman to be burned at Pontoise, in despite of all prayers, and so she was, and justice was done in public."

William of Chartres writes: "By his royal authority he repressed the insolence of many seigneurs, who were eager to despoil their poor subjects." The counsels given to his son, already quoted by us, indicate a preference, at any rate provisional, for doing justice to the weaker side, and from this we can to some extent infer a general preference for the lower classes in his policy; but only in doubtful cases and in open questions, for when his conscience was fully satisfied and the truth confirmed, he was not a man to deviate from his maxim of absolute justice for all: "Do that which is right."

In his time, and a little earlier, by an impulse of natural ascent, an intermediate class had arisen from the lower orders, intermediate between them and the seignorial aristocracy, namely *the bourgeoisie*, which was itself divided into several classes and orders, three of which may be distinguished. There was the *bourgeoisie* of the *communes*; these, in virtue of charters obtained or wrested from the seigneurs, formed in many respects little republics, administering their own laws, and enjoying an independence resembling that of seignorial fiefs; the more substantial citizens, enriched by commerce, were sometimes able to constitute an aristocratic and very oppressive oligarchy in these communes. There was the *bourgeoisie* of the merely *good towns*, not invested with communal privileges, but provided with what was called customary charters, that is, very extensive rights and civil franchises. There was finally a *bourgeoisie* properly called royal, an able creation of the Capet dynasty; the rights and privileges enjoyed by the "king's citizen" had a personal character, and followed him to whatever place in which he chose to live.

In the case of these different classes of citizens, as in the case of all his other subjects, St Louis, as we cannot too often repeat, was the guardian and defender of acquired rights, the arbiter in opposing interests, the protector of the weak, the zealous advocate of reason, order and justice. It may be asked whether his invariable principles of equity were combined with a very legitimate desire to maintain the political equilibrium, and even to secure the superiority by considering the *bourgeoisie* as a support necessary to uphold and strengthen the kingship against the feudal aristocracy. The reply to this question cannot be doubtful when we considered the following passage in the *Instructions*, as it is given in the text adopted by Joinville. " You must take care that your followers and subjects live under you in peace and uprightness. Above all, keep the good towns and the communes of the kingdom in the same condition and freedom in which they have been kept by your forefathers; if there is anything to be amended, amend and restore it, and hold them in love and favour; for by reason of the power and riches of the great cities, your subjects and foreigners will fear to do anything against you, and especially your peers and barons." But this passage is of doubtful authenticity, and has been disputed. It must, however, be borne in mind that it is in a chronicle composed at St Denis that this counsel is first found as part of the text of the *Instructions*, and that Matthew of Vendôme, abbot of St Denis, who died in 1286, had been one of St Louis's most trusted counsellors, since the pious king chose him for one of the regents of the kingdom during his Tunis crusade. We can hardly err in considering the passage as at any rate an important reflection or echo of the inward thoughts and confidential words of St Louis, even although it may not be entitled to the place which has perhaps been arbitrarily given to it in the precious document composed for Prince Philip.

With respect to the people, and especially to the agricultural class, it is not doubtful that St Louis's reign was peculiarly beneficial, owing to the general principles of justice and peace by which his government was regulated. His personal action is clearly seen, not merely in his lavish almsgiving and numerous charitable foundations, but also in the special care with which he protected the humble and necessary toil of the labourer, the life and security of the peasant, against the habitual consequences of armed strife. The interference with the work of tillage was, as we have seen, one of the chief evils to which he sought to put an end by prohibiting private feuds. The *Instructions* to his son show in a still more touching manner how much he had at heart this protection of the poor. " If it become needful for you to make war, be very careful that the poor people who had no part in the injustice which led to it should be preserved from all hurt, either by fire or otherwise, for it is better that you should constrain the ill-doer by seizing his goods, his towns and castles, than that you should ravage the goods of the poor." St Louis's popularity was genuine, and had, perhaps, something to do with the strange crusade of the *pastoureaux* in 1251. He was truly loved by his people, because he truly loved them.

There was, however, a small section of his subjects who inspired the holy king with a deep sense of mistrust, and he was disposed to act rigorously towards them, since he considered their doctrines and actions to be dangerous to the religious faith and morality of his people, and as hostile to the very foundations of Christian society: the heretics and the Jews. "Do what you can," he told his son, "to expel heretics from the land, as well as other evil people, so that it may be thoroughly purged; do whatever you are able in this matter by the good counsel of wise and discreet men." The terms of this counsel show a thoughtful moderation in practice, from which, indeed, the wise king does not appear to have deviated. The words "Keep the Jews in great subjection," which appear in this place in one of the versions of the *Instructions*, are among the most disputed passages. They do, indeed, correspond with St Louis's real sentiments, yet his policy towards the Jews settled in his dominions differed from that of his predecessors and successors, since it was not inspired by a desire of religious persecution or of fiscal gain, but on the one hand by a feeling of vigilance and precaution against secret cabalistic practices opposed to Christianity, and on the other hand against the arbitrary and excessive usury exacted by this people which had been chosen of God and then rejected. His faith, as learned as it was zealous, was not ignorant of the invincible persistence of this race, of its special claims to life, and of its future conversion, and he took pleasure as we have seen in the furtherance of its first fruits by gentle means. In taking measures of precaution and rigour, he sought then and always to establish justice and peace for all his people.

CHAPTER IV

FOREIGN POLICY

PEACE and justice were the two chief motives of St Louis's foreign policy, that is, of his relations with contemporary Christian rulers. " Dear son," he writes in his *Instructions*, " I enjoin you to refrain as far as possible from war with any other Christian power. And if you are wronged by any one, try in many ways to find some means of asserting your rights without being obliged to go to war."

In giving this counsel St Louis shows that there was nothing pusillanimous in his love of peace. This is confirmed by his practice. The vigorous campaign in Poitou and Saintonge had sufficed to show the king of England that St Louis was not a man to flinch from the necessary defence of his rights and legitimate interests. The concessions which he thought it right to make to Henry III. in the treaty of Paris (May 28, 1258), which was ratified in London in the following year, were, as he believed, notwithstanding the remonstrances of his advisers, a transaction favourable to his kingdom, as well as consonant to his just and pacific spirit.

"Those on the council," writes Joinville, " were much opposed to this peace, and spoke thus to him: ' Sire, we greatly marvel that you should be willing to give the king of England such a large portion of the land which you and your forefathers conquered from him, and which he renounced. If you believe that you have no right to it, you do not make full restitution to the king of England unless you give up all that was conquered by you and your forefathers; and if you believe that you have a right to it, we think that you are throwing away all that you surrender.'

"To these words the holy king replied in this manner: 'Seigneurs, I am certain that the forefathers of the king of England justly lost the conquest which I hold, and as for the land which I give up, I do not give it to him and his heirs because I am bound to do so, but that there may be love between my children and his, who are cousins. And it seems to me that I do well to make this gift, since he was not before this my vassal, and must now do homage to me.'"

M. Lecoy de la Marche makes the following reflections on the subject: "Many historians have accused St Louis of yielding to excessive scruples on this point. A serious examination of the tenor of the treaty, of the situation which dictated the stipulations, and of that which ensued from it, leads to a quite opposite conclusion. The king of England had for several years never ceased to claim the provinces wrested from him by Philip Augustus; he might come to assert that right by arms, and it was easy to foresee the disasters which might ensue, besides the miseries inseparable from such a war. Unless the victory were complete, half the patrimony so laboriously acquired must be renounced. In case of a reverse, two or three small seigneuries would not be lost, but the fruitful Normandy, Touraine, Anjou, Poitou, and all which had formerly belonged to the Plantagenets. To prevent the possibility of such mutilation at the cost of a slight sacrifice, was an act of foresight altogether worthy of a prince who wished to keep nothing by violence, but who, in his own case as in that of others, sought to secure the consent of the adverse party. When we come to consider in what the sacrifice consisted, we find that there was no cession of suzerainty or nationality. The ceded territories remained French, and were only joined to the duchy of Guyenne in order to be held with it as a fief. Not only must homage be paid to him as liege lord, but it must also be paid for this latter duchy, which had not been the case before, and for all the king of England's possessions on the continent without distinction.

"So also with Bordeaux, Bayonne and Gascony, and all the lands on the further side of the English seas, in fiefs and domains and islands, if the king of England held any which were of the kingdom of France." The chronicler Primat puts the advantages of this clause in a very clear light. "For before this the land of Gascony did not depend on the kings of France, nor on their kingdom. And withal, it was so ordered that both the land which the king gave up and the land of Gascony should be held in homage as part of the kingdom of France from henceforth." This was an important fact; the sovereign of a powerful and rival nation became subordinate to the king of France, became his vassal, and in certain cases owed submission to him. We must be ill acquainted with the laws and usages of the feudal system if we see in this only an empty word, a purely honorary supremacy. The king of England placed himself in an attitude of real dependence; and so it was understood by St Louis, for, as we are told by Boutaric: " He maintained a French seneschal in Périgord, whose only occupation was to make the English agents in Guyenne aware of the supremacy of the king of France. The parliament of Paris received appeals against the sentences of English seneschals, and executed them by force. In 1269 a French seneschal seized the revenues of the king of England at Bordeaux, and at a later date Philip the Fair asserted his suzerainty over the king of England still more strongly."

In St Louis's opinion, and in fact, the treaty concluded with the king of England had two great advantages; by a peace concluded in good faith by both parties, it ended the period of open war which dated from the conquests of Philip Augustus from John Lackland, and had only been suspended by an occasional truce; by partial concessions on either side it also ensured these conquests to the crown of France, as the king of England himself admitted, and it formally placed that king in a position of dependence on France, so far as his possessions in that country were concerned. If the pious king's advisers thought him too conciliatory, the English barons accused Henry III. of having dishonoured himself by accepting conditions which they considered to be humiliating. St Louis's equity was, however, so generally recognised, and his prestige was so great, even in England, that he was chosen as arbiter by the king and barons in the dispute which arose between them with respect to the so-called Provisions of Oxford, drawn up to restrict the prerogatives of the English king. M. Wallon writes: "This step shows a great confidence in his uprightness. It was well known that he would not interfere in English affairs, like his father and grandfather, in order to seek his own advantage in the antagonism of parties; it was known that he would only aim at justice and the good of the country which had confidently appealed to his judgment. . . . He invited the kings and barons to meet him at Amiens. He went thither on January 13, 1264. Henry III., Eleanor, and several of the English barons went there also. . . . St Louis's judgment with respect to the decrees of Oxford was not doubtful. He was on the king's side, not because he was himself a king, but because the Oxford articles appeared to him to be destructive of all kingly authority. . . . The pious arbiter was perhaps in error in supposing that the prince to whom he restored his rights would understand his duties and behave in such cases as he would have behaved himself. In revoking the Oxford statutes, St Louis confirmed all the prior constitutions, but King John's Charter was included in these privileges, and the barons asserted that the Oxford articles were only the result of that Charter. St Louis's sentence, confirmed by the Pope, was therefore not ratified by the barons." At any rate his conscience bore witness that he had employed the efforts of a truly Christian diplomacy to preserve the rival kingdom, which had so lately been hostile, from the sufferings and exhaustion of a civil war.

This pacific spirit is also displayed in the holy king's attitude with respect to the terrible strife which began under Gregory VII. between the Papacy and the German emperors, who aspired to nothing less than the subjection of Italy, of the Holy See, and of the Church itself, to their domination. It was precisely in St Louis's time that this strife, which endured for ages, came to its height. Two great popes, Gregory IX. and Innocent IV., displayed an incomparable and victorious energy in opposition to the boldness and cunning of Frederic II., whose unbridled ambition, implacable anger, and licentious belief and morals, seriously threatened, not merely Italian independence and the liberty of the Church, but even the integrity of the Christian faith.

St Louis was placed at a somewhat different point of view, as it must be admitted, from that of the sovereign pontiffs, who, in the situation in which they stood, were more enlightened by special divine assistance, even without considering their infallibility, and they were convinced of the necessity of continuing to the end a conflict with an adversary whose detestable motives were less apparent to the pious monarch. He multiplied his loyal and charitable endeavours to bring about a reconciliation between Frederic and the Holy See, and his generous intervention was by no means censured by the Pope, who, on the contrary, considered it favourably, although without hope of success. The Head of the Church had, in fact, the consoling assurance that at the hour when the peril was imminent and manifest, the character of St Louis's intervention would promptly change. His energy was as little doubtful as his devotion. When, under Gregory IX., the French prelates who were on their way to the council convoked at Rome were seized at sea by the fleet of Pisa and kept prisoners by Frederic, "the king," as we are told by M. Elie Berger, "as soon as he heard what had happened, sent the abbot of Corbie and Gervais of Escrennes, one of the knights of his household, to demand their release from the emperor. Frederic thought fit to return a haughty and insulting refusal, and Louis at once sent a protest in which he went so far as to say: 'Our kingdom is not so weak that it must yield to a prick of the spur.'" And the prelates were released by the emperor. Again, under Innocent IV., when Frederic proposed to march upon Lyons,[1] where the Pope had taken refuge from the imperial forces then overpowering Italy, an appeal to the holy king was not made in vain. The same learned author writes: "In the middle of June 1247, Innocent IV. heard that the king of France had decided to defend him. Louis did not content himself with promising and raising troops; he prepared to set out in person. Blanche of Castile and her three other sons, following the king's example, were also ready to march to the help of the Holy See; the counts of Anjou, Poitiers, and Artois had already summoned their

[1] This city, not yet united to France, was at that time a free and independent town connected with the empire by a purely nominal tie.

knights. If the emperor crossed the Alps, all the forces of the French monarchy were to advance to the banks of the Saône and the Rhone." A revolt of the inhabitants of Parma compelled Frederic to renounce his design.

After the death of this formidable prince, whom St Louis had neither hated nor feared, he considered it to be in conformity with the interests of France, as well as to those of Christianity, to associate himself in an indirect but effective manner with the policy of the Holy See in Italy. We are told by M. Lecoy de la Marche : " That the best pledge which the king could give for this union was to accept the kingdom of Naples for his brother, Charles of Anjou, as a fief of the Holy See, since the popes, for very intelligible reason, would no longer leave it in possession of the emperors. He refused the investiture for one of his sons, since he was not ambitious for his family, and did not desire to infringe the rights of another house ; but considerations of general policy and the entreaties of Urban IV., whose French origin added to his influence, induced him to accept it for his brother. He even sent troops to his aid ; he allowed Charles to levy tithes in France in order to facilitate the conquest of the kingdom from his competitor Manfred ; he caused a crusade to be preached against the latter, in which he himself took part. We cannot, however, suppose that he approved of the severity with which Charles of Anjou carried on the government in Naples and Sicily, nor of the execution of Frederic's grandson, the young Conradin, which, while completing the ruin of the German rule, led to that of the French dynasty in Italy. Such acts were inconsistent with his character, and could not have his assent. But Charles had not maintained towards the head of his house the deference and submission which were shown to him by his other brother, Alphonse of Poitiers, in the acts of his administration; he carried out his own independent policy, a policy which in Sicily led to the terrible massacre known as the Sicilian Vespers. This disaster might have been averted if the holy king had lived, or if his influence had still directed the course of events which gradually led up to these bloody reprisals."

Transactions which by means of mutual concession brought pretensions hitherto in dispute to a satisfactory end, were the cherished policy of St Louis. He concluded a treaty of this nature with the king of Aragon in the same month as that with the king of England. M. Wallon writes: " France claimed the suzerainty of Roussillon and of Barcelona, since they had formed part of Charlemagne's empire, and up to the time of Philip Augustus the reigns of the kings of France were noted in the public acts. On the other hand, the kings of Aragon claimed rights on great part of the provinces which stretch to the north-east of the Pyrenees, or along the Mediterranean: Limoux, Carcassonne, Narbonne, Bèziers, Agde, Nîmes, Gévaudan, Albigeois, Ronergue, Quercy, the county of Foix, and even the county of Toulouse. The king of Aragon was anxious to come to an agreement, and St Louis showed himself ready to comply. The king of France renounced the sovereignty of Catalonia, the king of Aragon abandoned all the claims just enumerated, and all rights which had formerly pertained to the county of Toulouse. The negotiation was concluded at Corbeil, May 1, 1258, on the same day as the marriage of St Louis' son with the daughter of James I.

Either in the case of foreign princes or of the great seigneurs of his kingdom, St Louis, whenever it was possible, sought to put an end to disputes, whether he had any interest in them or not. Joinville writes: " He was, of all men in the world, the most intent on making peace between his subjects, and especially between the rich men in the neighbourhood and the princes of the kingdom, as for instance between the Count of Chalon, uncle to the seigneur of Joinville, and his son, the Count of Burgundy, who had a great feud when we returned from over sea. In order to make peace between the father and son, he sent men of his council to Burgundy at his own cost, and by his endeavours peace was made between the father and son.

" There was afterwards a great strife between the King Thibaut of Champagne and Count John of Chalon, and the Count of Burgundy, his son, for the abbey of Luxeuil. To pacify this strife, the king sent Gervais of Escrennes, who was at that time *maître queux* of France, and by his efforts he made a reconciliation between them.

" After the king had composed this dispute, there was another great strife between Count Thibaut of Bar and Count Henry of Luxembourg, who had married Thibaut's sister, and it fell out that they fought against each other near Prény, and Henry of Luxembourg was taken prisoner by Thibaut of Bar, and he took possession of the castle of Ligny, which came to the Count of Luxembourg through his wife. To compose this war, the king sent his chamberlain, Monseigneur Peter, whom of all men in the world he trusted most, and it was at the king's expense; and a reconciliation was made by the king's efforts.

"With respect to those foreigners reconciled by the king, some of his council said that he did amiss in not leaving them to fight; for if he left them to become impoverished, they would not attack him as soon as they were very rich. And to this the king replied, and said that they spoke amiss: 'for if the neighbouring princes saw that I wished to let them fight, they might take counsel together and say it is out of malice that the king let us fight. Then it might be that from their hatred of me they would come to attack me, and I might be worsted, without counting that I should incur the hatred of God, who has said: 'Blessed are the peacemakers.'

"Whence it came to pass that the Burgundians and the Lorrainers, whom he had reconciled, loved and obeyed him, so that I saw them come to plead before the king in causes they had among themselves in the king's court at Rheims, Paris and Orleans."

Thus, even from the merely human point of view, the holy king had no reason to regret that as the inspiration and leading principle of his government and policy, he had at once chosen and constantly obeyed the words of the angels at the Messiah's birth: "Glory to God in the highest, on earth peace and goodwill towards men."

CHAPTER V

A COMPARISON BETWEEN ST LOUIS'S VIRTUES AS A PRIVATE INDIVIDUAL AND A KING—THE GENERAL CHARACTERISTICS AND RESULTS OF HIS REIGN

LOUIS IX. was a saint, both as man and king. It will not be unprofitable, after considering his virtues and merits from this double point of view, for an observer who wishes to estimate as clearly as possible the true character of such a man and such a prince, to consider the relation which his private and kingly qualities bear to each other.

Among the noble and heroic virtues which became every day more distinctive and significant in this elect soul, his grand and deeply seated habits of personal religion, of equity and charity, were, as we cannot doubt, the pure source and fruitful principle of his incomparable reign. It was St Louis's religion, that is, his understanding and practice of the Gospel, which, speaking literally, in his quality, so lovingly embraced, of a disciple of Jesus Christ, attached him to his duty towards God, whence his duty towards his people had its source. St Louis's government is one of the noblest historic testimonies in favour of the Christian faith.

The somewhat severe equity which we have seen to be one of the most striking features of his moral character is certainly a king's virtue. The unction of the Gospel, combined with his natural kindness of heart, moderated without weakening it, and made it still more kingly. The union of charity and firmness which appears in the conduct and decisions of St Louis is that of a man who has the cross graven on his heart, but who also holds the sceptre, and who knows how to do an act of justice as well as of devotion. We may note on this point a curious anecdote of the return from his crusade, due, like so many others, to Joinville:

"After leaving the island of Lampedusa, we saw a large island in the sea, called Pantenelia, and peopled by Saracens who were subject to the kings of Sicily and Tunis. The queen asked the king to send three galleys to procure fruit for her children, and the king consented, and gave orders to the masters of the galleys to be ready to come to him when they saw the king's ship passing before the island. The galleys entered a port in order to land on the island, and so it was that when the king's ship passed before the port, we had no news of the galleys.

"The sailors began to murmur one to another. The king sent for them and asked what they thought of this matter, and the sailors said that they thought that the Saracens had taken the galleys and their crews. 'But, sire, we give you the advice and counsel not to await them, for you are between the kingdom of Sicily and the kingdom of Tunis, and are by no means beloved by either; and if you let us set sail we shall deliver you from peril while it is still dark, for we shall bring you through this strait.'

"'Truly,' said the king, 'I cannot believe that you would have me leave my followers in the hands of the Saracens without doing all that is possible to save them, and I command you to shift the sails and make for the island.' And when the queen heard this she began to show great grief, and to say, 'Alas! it is I who have done this.'

"While they shifted the sails of the king's ships and of the others, we saw the galleys coming from the island. When they came close to the king, he asked the sailors why they had tarried, and they answered that they could not help it, and that it was the fault of the sons of the citizens of Paris, six of whom ate the fruits of the gardens, so that the sailors could not bring them away, and did not wish to leave them. Then the king ordered them to be placed in the skiff, and then they began to cry and shout: 'Sire, for God's sake, take from us all that we have, but do not put us in the place in which thieves and murderers are kept, for it will always be a reproach to us.'

"The queen and all of us did what we could to make the king desist, but the king would listen to no one; they were put into the skiff, and there remained until we landed. They were in such danger that when the sea rose the waves flew over their heads, and they had to crouch down for fear the wind should sweep them into the sea. And this was just, for their gluttony did us such damage that we were delayed for full eight days, since the king caused the vessels to be put back."

The virtue of charity, so eminent in St Louis, was

also displayed by him in a kingly manner. It is to this that we must ascribe his pacific spirit, of which we have noted such noble efforts in his internal government and foreign policy, and to this also is due the favour shown to the weak, which made his rule formidable to oppressors and a sort of earthly providence and a faithful image of the goodness of God. As we have already observed, his foundations and almsgiving had not merely the merit of personal beneficence, but to a large extent a character of public interest, especially if we consider the social condition of that period. Although lavish, they did not injure the good economy of his finances, which was maintained without overburdening his people, nor yet that splendour of royal dignity which is in some cases necessary. On this point a sort of equilibrium and ingenious compensation was established in his conscience and conduct. Geoffrey of Beaulieu writes: "Aware that some of his followers murmured at his lavish almsgiving, he told them that since it was impossible to avoid some excess in his expenditure, he wished this excess to be in the alms given for love of our Lord rather than in secular and mundane things; so that the excess in things spiritual might excuse and make amends for the excess in mundane things which it was impossible to avoid. And yet," the pious biographer adds, " he acted largely and liberally in solemnities, parliaments, and assemblies of knights and barons, as beseemed his royal dignity, and his court was ordered with still greater care and majesty than that of the kings his predecessors."

THE KING

The transcendent fervour of his religious zeal, of his active piety, and superhuman asceticism might at a first glance appear to be more in contradiction than in conformity with his royal functions. He was not secure from reproaches on this point, and on one occasion they took the form of a public insult. Queen Margaret's confessor writes: "A woman called Sarrette was pleading in the pious king's court against a knight whose name was John of Fouilleuse. Now one day, when the parliament was held in Paris, as the pious king came out of his chamber, this woman, who was at the foot of the stairs, said to him: 'Fie, fie! You ought not to be king of France. It would be much better to have another king, for you are ever busied with minor friars, with preaching friars, with priests and clerks; it is a great pity that you are king of France, and it is a great marvel that you have not been put out of the kingdom.' And when the pious king's sergeants wished to beat the woman and chase her out, he said and gave orders that she should not be beaten nor sent away, and he spoke and answered smiling: 'Certainly you speak the truth, I am unworthy to be king, and if it pleased our Lord, it would have been better that another should have been king who knew better how to govern the kingdom'; and then the pious king told one of his chamberlains to give money to this woman, as it is believed, forty *sous*; and many persons were present when these things were said."

This charming act of clemency and humility does not imply that St Louis admitted the objections made to his zeal and fervour to be well founded. On the contrary, his conscience firmly asserted a right to the sublime enjoyment of supernatural order and divine love as part of his happiness on earth, and a compensation for the heavy burden of supreme power, as it was understood and practised by him with constant care for the welfare of his people at the expense of his natural taste for contemplation, study, penitence and prayer. If he was content to smile at Sarrette's exaggerated complaints, he offered a direct and sarcastic reply to the disobliging remarks current about him among barons of a mundane spirit. Geoffrey of Beaulieu writes: "As he had heard that some of the nobles murmured against him because he heard so many masses and sermons, he replied that if he were to employ twice as much time in dice-throwing, or in ranging through the forest to hunt animals and birds, no one would make objection."

And indeed St Louis's ascetic and transcendent virtues did not interfere with his duties as a sovereign. Since absolute perfection is not to be found in man, his fervent zeal may have drawn him into some illusions and exaggerated acts. But on the other hand, it was from this ever flowing source that he derived his strong and pure devotion, his absolute abandonment to his royal mission, that is, to safeguarding the rights and interests of others, to which he sacrificed his rest, his health, and life itself. The extraordinary manifestations of his Christian heroism, at once sincere and spontaneous, surround his brow and diadem, even in his lifetime, with an aureole which increased his power. As we are told by William of Chartres: "Many were astonished, and some of his ill-wishers complained that so humble and peaceable a man, neither strong in body nor severe in action, should thus exert a pacific domination over so great a kingdom, and so many great and powerful seigneurs. . . . This cannot be ascribed to earthly power, but to divine virtue." And Geoffrey of Beaulieu writes: "All his subjects, high and low, held him in respect and fear, because of his justice and saintliness."

St Louis's piety rested on the foundation of a truly enlightened faith, a steadfast morality and admirable good sense, to which he added those careful practices of the catholic faith which were dear and familiar to him, and which are so profitable to those by whom they are fully understood. In this he differed from some princes of earlier times, as for instance from Charlemagne's simple and fanciful heir, who was called Louis the Pious by his contemporaries, an epithet not unjustly changed by posterity into Louis the Courteous, whose devotion was childish and pusillanimous. Neither was St Louis's devotion like that of his contemporary Henry III. of England, external and formal, although sincere; it is said that Henry heard at least as many masses as St Louis, that he dispersed lavish alms, that he visited the sick, and even kissed lepers, and yet was so far from being a saint that he was not even a wise man, still less a great king. The vehement fervour of St Louis's religion did not affect the clearness of his mind and the firmness of his will, and it is noteworthy, as we see in certain difficult questions of his government and policy, that his conscience as a king, while always truly Christian and devoted to the Church and the Holy See, was in some sense more liberal than his conscience as a man and simple believer, which was perhaps sometimes rather timid. Being a king, it was as a king that he thought and acted. His devotion was no hindrance to him, but rather a support.

The question of the general agreement of his private virtues and heroic asceticism with his royal qualities is set at rest by the characteristics and results of his reign. The reign of Louis the Pious led the way to the division of Charlemagne's empire; the reign of St Louis consolidated and developed the kingdom and kingship of Philip Augustus and the dynasty of Hugh Capet, caused it to be generally respected and accepted, and finally raised it to pre-eminence in the Christian world. He gave to internal France, which up to that time was a prey to the terrible strife of princely rivals and to the bloody anarchy of feudal turbulence, order, equilibrium, peace and prosperity.[1] He made France great in her foreign relations. Even his reverses established

[1] It is to St Louis's reign that we must ascribe the merit of the remarkable prosperity enjoyed by France until towards the middle of the fourteenth century. Siméon Luce, in his history of Bertrand du Guesclin and his time, writes: "There can be no doubt that during the first half of the fourteenth century, before the plagues of 1348 and the first disasters of the so-called hundred years' war, the population of France equalled if it did not exceed that of modern France. We propose to show that this increase of population corresponded with a general prosperity to which our country has probably not attained again until quite recently."

French influence in the East. A Tartar khan once asked a religious missionary: "Who is the greatest Western prince?" The missionary, still imbued with the ideas of earlier times, replied: "The Emperor." "You are wrong," said the savage chief, "it is the King of France." Without violence and without injustice he exalted the kingly power to an effective, and indeed to an ideal height, whence it seems that the law and dominant idea directed the course of history through the ages, and in spite of the most cruel reverses, up to the time of the crisis, not yet concluded, which marked the end of last century. M. Paul Viollet writes: "The ascendency exercised by St Louis undoubtedly contributed to the development of the central authority. This king, whose moral greatness and military power had raised him to such a height among Christian princes, had also attained to an authority over his own kingdom which was unknown to his predecessors, an authority by which his successors benefited." The destinies of the French monarchy may be said to have been decided by the humble and penitent ascetic who knelt down to serve the poor leprous monk of the abbey of Royaumont.

CHAPTER VI

ST LOUIS, AS HE APPEARED TO HIS OWN AGE AND TO POSTERITY

AS M. Wallon has justly remarked, St Louis sought first the kingdom of God and His justice, but, in accordance with the divine promise, the rest was abundantly given to him. He stands supreme above the sovereigns of his time, and before his royal form that of Henry III. of England and of the Emperor Frederic II. must fade, since the natural gifts of the latter were spoiled by ambition and unbridled vice. The pure and sublime form of St Louis has remained in the eyes of history at the centre and summit of the grand epoch which marks the apogee of the Middle Ages. As the seventeenth century is the age of Louis XIV., so the thirteenth century is the age of St Louis. The ascetic, knightly and royal figure whose brow wears the aureole of the blessed, as well as the unction of a king, is in manifest agreement with all which is noble and good in the civilisation of that day, in spite of the imperfections from which no period of the history of mankind is exempt.

No architecture could have been better suited to St Louis's effusive piety than the marvels of religious and Christian art which passed during his reign from the austere elegance of the *lanciate* style into the efflorescence of the later Gothic, which may be said to spiritualise even stone work. It became every day more docile to the daring spirit of the architects and to the strong and able hand of sculptors, as if proud to form the framework of the edifying and instructive glass windows. St Louis directly contributed to the development of Gothic art by his numerous constructions, and in particular by building the *Sainte Chapelle*, that enchanting and expressive work of French art in the Middle Ages, and of the holy king's devotion. Jean de Jaudun writes: "What shall we say of this chapel, built early in the fourteenth century? It seems to lurk modestly behind the walls of the royal dwelling, as remarkable for the solidity and perfection of its construction as for its brilliant colouring, for the pictures which stand out from a gold background, the transparent glory of its stained glass, the decoration of its altars, and the splendid reliquaries set with precious stones. On entering the church we seem to be taken up to heaven, and into one of the fairest chambers of Paradise."

A considerable part of Notre Dame was built in St Louis's reign; he certainly contributed to its cost, and is directly commemorated, as we are told by M. Lecoy de la Marche, in a compartment of the red door, which contains four very interesting figures, those of St Louis and the queen, his wife, kneeling before our Saviour and the Blessed Virgin. The tomb of the young Prince Louis must also be included in the monuments of the art of that time; he was the holy king's eldest son, and died in 1260. The same author writes: "The recumbent figure of this monument expresses placid innocence, as of one who has fallen asleep on the bosom of the Saviour, and the monks who fill the niches present matter for careful study in the variety of their attitude and expression." At St Denis, St Louis restored Dagobert's tomb in the taste of the thirteenth century, and between 1230 and 1240 it is said that he renewed the statues of those kings, his predecessors, who are buried in this celebrated church.

He held profane music in slight esteem, and kept it away from his palace, except at solemn banquets, but he had a passion for sacred music which seems to have had some influence on the progress of harmony. " His choir, well mounted, gave its tone to others; and even through the miseries of the crusade, he had musicians with him to enhance the splendour of worship given in his tent to the God of hosts. It seems that he could not dispense with them, for we learn from William of Nangis that during his pilgrimage to Nazareth, which was made in two days, mass, vespers and matins were sung solemnly and gloriously, accompanied by the organ and stringed instruments, as we learn from those who were present."

We have already given a special account of St Louis's intellectual qualities and customs. They were altogether directed to ecclesiastical and doctrinal literature, and detached from profane literature, both popular and aristocratic. Yet his glorious and pacific reign was by no means ineffectual for the maintenance and development of the domination then exercised in Europe by the French language and poetry, and it was undoubtedly as the capital of his kingdom, as well as the site of the most flourishing schools of Christendom, that Paris achieved the extraordinary renown and influence which were everywhere accorded to her. M. Léon Clédat writes: "France alone enjoyed the benefits of a wise and scrupulously conscientious government, anxious for general peace and for the happiness of all, and strictly just. . . . At this time French nearly became the definitive language of England, for it made great progress, even among the common people, and but for the hundred years' war, it seems probable that English would have become only a patois. Well-born English writers made use of French. Brunetto Latino chose the same language in which to write his encyclopedia *Le Trésor*, and he gives the following reason for his choice: 'Although we are Italians, this book is written in the French romance language, because the French mode of speaking is the most delectable, and in the most common use.' Since the Roman conquest there has been no parallel to this diffusion of our language. . . .

"Paris assumed the dominant position which she has not ceased to keep, and which has made her from that time the capital of letters and of the arts. In the wonderful development of architecture and of monumental sculpture which characterises the thirteenth century, the school of the Isle of France had, as Viollet-le-Duc has noted, a marked superiority. . . . With respect to literature, while the different provinces of France continued to produce poets and prose writers of talent, the language of the Isle of France prevailed more and more over the neighbouring dialects, and the provincial writers excused themselves for not speaking correct Parisian French. Finally, Paris was above all the city of vigorous learning. Students flocked thither from all parts of the civilised world; some of these became teachers in their turn, and were honoured by being professors in the University which had formed them. The Pope Alexander IV. writes in 1256: ' Paris fills the universe with the fulness of her knowledge; she diffuses the light of intelligence, disperses the darkness of ignorance, and reveals the secrets of learning to the world. She is the city renowned for letters and science, the foremost school of erudition.' Alexander IV. was not content to celebrate the glory of Paris; he sent his two nephews there, and thus proved the sincerity of his praise.

"Among the celebrated foreigners who studied or taught in Paris, or who resided there, we may mention Albert the Great, Bacon, *the admirable doctor*, St Buonaventura and St Thomas of Aquinas; the Italian chronicler Fra Salimbene, the 'spiritual vagabond,' and his fellow-countryman, John of Parma, who was not the author but the responsible publisher of the *Eternal Gospel*, Brunetto Latino, and finally the great poet Dante. . . . It was not only by arms and by instruction, but also by literature that we influenced the world, and this was in the Middle Ages, as in our own day, one chief cause of the diffusion of our language."

THE KING

Among the different branches of French literature in the Middle ages, the national store of dramatic songs, filled with the strife carried on by Charlemagne and Roland against the unbelieving Saracens, would not have been unworthy of St Louis's attention if it had retained its primitive character; but it had already fallen into complete decadence, and the legend which had early supplanted history was now itself replaced by purely fictitious inventions in which the holy king's sound judgment could take no pleasure. He was still less accessible to the fictions of the Round Table, and to poems of adventure in which the exaggerated and adventurous gallantry so ill accorded with the principles and precepts of Christian morality, and to this the aristocratic and courtly poetry of the *trouvères*, disciples of the troubadours of southern France, was equally opposed in the *chansons d'amour*, the most renowned of these lyric compositions. Religious inspiration had indeed its place in the narrative, lyric or didactic pieces of our poets. But the form was far from being as good as the substance, and its inadequacy must have failed to touch a mind nourished, like that of the pious king, on the strong meat of Scripture, of the Fathers and of the beauties of the liturgy. If Dante had been born in France, and in time to write his sublime epic vision in St Louis's reign, he might perhaps, with a certain reserve, have gained the attention and esteem of so good a judge for his able and poetic theology. But he was only born in 1265, and in Italy. Rutebeuf was a degraded clerk who became a *jongleur*, that is, a professional rhymer and reciter, a victim of his own recklessness and passion for dice, a frequenter of weddings and taverns, ever on the watch for some gift which did not always come; of a humour more satirical than religious, in spite of some religious songs and pious tales which were founded on a slender basis of theology and philosophy. If St Louis had occasion to observe Rutebeuf he would certainly have formed no favourable opinion of this poetry in the vulgar tongue which poured forth a copious flood of too facile rhymes, containing however, some lively traits of wit, and they were recited in the dwellings of seigneurs and citizens, and sometimes in the streets of the capital. These reflections did not spare the holy king himself, since the Parisian whose purse was always empty resented his liberal gifts, not to the *jongleurs*, but to the religious orders. Rutebeuf ever reproaches St Louis for his foundation of the *Quinze-Vingts*:

> Le roi a mis en un repaire
> Mais je ne sais pas pourquoi faire,
> Trois-cents aveugles côte-à-côte . . .
> Les uns tirent, les autres poussent,
> Et se donnent mainte secousse,
> Car n'y a nul qui les éclaire
> Si le feu y prenait, nul doute
> Que l'ordre ne fût tout brûlé :
> Aurait le roi plus à refaire.[1]

---

[1] The king has placed in a refuge, I know not why he did it, three hundred blind men side by side. Some pull, others push, for there is none to give them light, and they give each other many a shock. If the place caught fire, doubtless the whole order would be burnt and the king would have much to build again.

THE KING

Thank God, these light and ill-founded reflections fell short of their mark. The last word was with St Louis, not only in the opinion of the wise, but of the public. No canonisation was more clearly foreseen nor more welcome than that of the king. The Holy See, however favourably disposed, proceeded to make mature investigation under several successive pontificates, and especially with respect to the numerous miracles obtained by the intercession of the blessed king, whose bones had been brought from Tunis and buried at St Denis. After the canonisation, part of the relics of St Louis were transferred to the Sainte Chapelle. His heart, at the request of Charles of Anjou, was left in the abbey of Monreale, in Sicily.

The examination and discussion of the matter was so scrupulous and produced so many documents that, according to the report of one of the apostolic commissaries, Cardinal Benoît Cajetan, they exceeded an ass's load. This same cardinal, who was raised to the pontificate under the name of Boniface VIII. on the 11th August 1297, inscribed Louis IX. in the catalogue of saints, and sent the bull of canonisation to the bishops and archbishops of France.

The canonisation therefore took place in the reign of Philip the Fair. The sole connection of this prince's name with that of the pontiff who so willingly conferred this supreme honour on the holy king, sufficiently shows how much the spirit and policy of St Louis differed from those of his grandson. The striking difference between the two princes was a heart-felt sorrow to the survivors of that great reign. M. Gaston Paris writes: "Joinville has left in his memoirs unequivocal proofs of his want of sympathy with his new master. . . . As the friend of Louis IX., he wished all the descendants of the holy king to take him for a pattern. He says, in speaking of the canonisation, 'It is a great honour to all those of his line who wish to imitate him by their good actions, and a great dishonour to those who will not conform to his rule, a great dishonour, I say, to the ill-livers of his family; for men will point at them with the finger and say that the holy king, whose descendants they are, would never have done such evil acts.' This may be taken as a general warning, but other passages are absolutely clear. After repeating what St Louis had said of the profit to be drawn from an escape from great perils, which should be regarded as menaces from God to warn us of his wrath and of imminent punishment, he adds: 'May God preserve the present king, for he has escaped from as great peril as we did, and even greater; let him therefore amend his misdeeds, so that God may send no cruel blow on him, and on all that is his.' We see that Joinville, who especially admired in Louis IX. his perfect loyalty and his love of justice, felt nothing but dislike for a king who undoubtedly possessed great qualities but who made violence and cunning the principles of his government."

It was to St Louis that the nobles and the people of France appealed against the exactions of Philip the Fair. On the 14th May 1315, his successor, Louis X., made a solemn declaration that all things should be re-established in the state in which they were in the time of St Louis, and on the 29th January 1317, Philip the Tall renewed these fair promises. But the spirit of Philip the Fair, to the detriment of the honour and advantage of the French monarchy, continued through the succeeding centuries to intermingle in varying degrees with the spirit of St Louis, still to a large extent apparent in the traditional and truly national work of his dynasty, and in the government of his most worthy successors. The disasters of the hundred years' war almost destroyed this work and dynasty, but the heavenly guardianship of St Louis was not wanting to France. His name, as the heroic maid herself bears witness, is closely connected with the mission of Joan of Arc. Cousinot de Montreuil, the author of the *Chronique de la Pucelle*, writes: "One day Joan wished to speak privately to the king, Charles VII., and said to him, 'Gentle dauphin, why do you doubt me? I tell you that God has pity on you, your kingdom and your people; for St Louis and St Charlemagne kneel before him, praying for you; and I tell you this thing, which will show that you ought to believe me.'"

Towards the end of the Middle Ages, the still living popularity of St Louis is shown by the composition and representations of two dramatic mysteries in his honour. The second, a work not without interest, by a poet whose fame has been revived, chiefly owing to the unhistoric fancies of Victor Hugo, bears the following title in the original manuscript: "Here begins the life of Monseigneur Saint Louis, King of France, with personages, composed by

Master Peter Gringoire, at the request of the
Masters and Governors of the confraternity of the
said Saint Louis, founded in the chapel of St Blaise,
in Paris." This was a confraternity of the masons
and carpenters of Paris, of which the patrons were
St Blaise, bishop and martyr, and St Louis, king of
France; the chapel is in Rue Galande, near the
Church of St Julian the Poor. We find in the
eighth book of this mystery how the news of the
holy king's death was received in France, mixed,
according to custom in the later compositions of
this character, with real, symbolical and allegorical
personages.

The People. Now we know not in what place is
our king and valiant prince. It is long since news
of him came to the country of France. May the
high and immortal Power protect him in time of
need.

Good Counsel. We are all subject to death. Doubt
not, O people, that Louis, the good king of France,
who has kept peace in his own time, has passed out
of this world and has left his son Philip to lead his
noble array.

The People. Alas, the good king! He maintained
the laws. He observed justice faithfully, according
to law, right and reason.

Good Counsel. Alas! the good king! The whole
church militant has been wise and flourishing, peaceable and at rest during his time.

The People. Alas! the good king! He upheld
citizens, merchants, even the tillers of the land;
he punished the disorderly, the pillagers and thieves.

THE KING

Good Counsel. Alas! the good king! He supported the simple and ignorant, he comforted the poor and beggars; he kept the faith of Jesus and the fear of God.

The People. Alas! the good king!

This is not the place for considering the good and evil aspects of the Renascence, its real advantages and still more certain drawbacks, but one of its worst results was that of producing in political affairs a deplorable tendency to the scepticism of Macchiavelli, and in things intellectual a blind taste for Pagan antiquity, a twofold and serious injury to the mind, to tradition and even to the fame of St Louis. Detached from its real surroundings, his essentially Christian and French character was no longer so well understood and appreciated. The historian, Pierre Mathieu, absurdly confers upon him the favour of Jove. Pierre Lemoyne, of the Company of Jesus, in his heroic poem of eighteen cantos (1653), has at any rate the merit of choosing a subject which serves as a protest against the exclusive spirit which devoted our whole literature to Greek and Roman literature. Yet, as if in spite of himself, he was so dominated by the classical spirit that he surrounds the holy king with the strangest medley of Olympus, Parnassus, and the heroic and comic fairy tales of Ariosto and Tasso. In Boileau's fine work (1669) he seeks to turn the ambition of Louis XIV. from his unfortunate passion for war and conquest, and we find the following passage:

" There is more than one glory. It is a vain error to place victorious kings in the first rank, for these are the most common among great heroes. Every age is fertile in successful and daring men; every climate produces the favourites of Mars; the Seine has its Bourbons, the Tiber its Cæsars. We have seen a thousand times victorious Goths and Vandals issue from the marshes of Meotides, but we must run through all history to find a king who is truly a king; one who makes his plans wisely, and who can keep his subjects in peace and happiness. Earth counts few of such beneficent kings, and Heaven takes a long while to form them."

Here we might expect St Louis's name. Not at all; it is Titus whom he proposes as an example to Louis XIV.

"Such was the Emperor in whose reign the Rome which he adored saw the days of Saturn and of Rhea return."

The memory of the best and most Christian of our kings could not, however, be effaced in France under his descendants. When critical learning was applied to our annals, and the national history began to be scrutinised with the same care and rigorous methods which had been used in the case of Greek and Roman antiquity, the fame of St Louis was necessarily revived. Du Cange and Le Nain de Tillemont were busied in throwing light on the exact characteristics of his life and times. Tillemont's work was indeed only published in our own day, but Filleau de la Chaise made use of it in his life of St Louis (1688), now forgotten, but not without its use at that time. The image of his august ancestor was, moreover, not so completely absent from the mind of Louis XIV.

as his errors might lead us to suppose; always French and royal, and at last seriously and firmly Christian, the influence of Madame de Maintenon doubtless contributed to revive it. This seems to be shown by two acts which would not have been disavowed by St Louis—the creation of the order of chivalry which was destined to reward military merit, and which bore the name and was under the patronage of the holy king, and the foundation of the great house of Saint Cyr for the education of girls of good family, which bore the official title of the Royal Institution of St Louis, and its teachers were in 1694 formed into a regular congregation under the name of the *Dames de St Louis*. It was in the chapel of this house that Bourdaloue delivered the remarkable panegyric called the Sermon for the Feast of St Louis. Notwithstanding some historical errors, intelligible in that age, this sermon is, taken as a whole, quite worthy of the great Jesuit's accurate reason. We give the *proposition* as it was set forth by the orator:

"It is a sentiment, my fellow Christians, very injurious to Providence to suppose that there are in the world any conditions absolutely opposed to saintliness, or that saintliness is in itself incompatible with certain conditions and certain states of which it is nevertheless admitted that God is the author. To disabuse you of so dangerous an error, it is enough to put before you the example of St Louis; and this is the complete proof of what I propose to establish in this discourse for your instruction and for the edification of your souls. St Louis, when on earth, was a great king and a great saint; it is therefore possible to be a saint in all states and conditions of the world; this argument is sensible and convincing, for if there is in the world a condition difficult to combine with saintliness, it is evidently that of a king, as you will yourselves admit. And yet, thanks to God's providence, the kingship did not hinder St Louis from attaining to an eminent saintliness; nor did the eminent saintliness to which St Louis attained hinder him from fulfilling worthily the duties of his kingship. I say further; it was the kingship which rendered St Louis capable of such exalted saintliness, and it was his saintliness which enabled him to maintain the kingship in such honour. In two words, St Louis was a great saint because, being born a king, he had the gift to make his dignity of service to his saintliness: this will be the first part; St Louis was a great king because, in becoming a saint, he made his saintliness of service to his dignity: this will be the second part. From these two truths I shall draw for our consolation, two consequences equally touching and edifying; one, that to whatever state of life we are called is, in the order of divine predestination, that which will contribute most to sanctify us before God; the other, that our sanctification before God is the most certain and efficacious of all means to render us perfect and irreproachable in the estimation of the world, in that state to which we are called. It is a king who will teach us both these truths; therefore attend."

Louis XV. and the eighteenth century unhappily went far astray from the life of St Louis and the teaching of Bourdaloue. Yet the philosophy of that age, enlightened by the progress of learning, could not refrain from doing homage to the royal virtues of Louis IX., although he had been canonised. In his *Essai sur les Mœurs*, Voltaire writes: " Louis IX. appeared to be a prince destined to reform Europe, if she could have been reformed, to render France triumphant and civilised, and to be in all things a pattern for men. His piety, which was that of an anchorite, did not deprive him of any kingly virtue. A wise economy took nothing from his liberality. A profound policy was combined with strict justice, and he is perhaps the only sovereign which is entitled to this praise; prudent and firm in counsel, intrepid without rashness in his wars, he was as compassionate as if he had always been unhappy. No man could have carried virtue further."

PRINTED BY
TURNBULL AND SPEARS,
EDINBURGH

THE SAINTS

The Series is under the General Editorship of

M. HENRI JOLY,

formerly Professor at the Sorbonne and at the Collège de France, author of numerous works upon Psychology, and the authorised English translations are having, and will continue to have, the advantage of the revision of the

REV. FATHER TYRRELL, S.J.,

who contributes to each volume a Preface, and, in some cases, a few notes addressed especially to English readers.

Volumes already issued:

THE PSYCHOLOGY OF THE SAINTS
S. VINCENT DE PAUL   S. AUGUSTINE
S. CLOTILDA   S. IGNATIUS OF LOYOLA
S. LOUIS

New Volume now ready

S. IGNATIUS OF LOYOLA

By HENRI JOLY, Author of "The Psychology of the Saints."

Catholic Times.—"M. Joly has taken up his theme with that earnest desire to be clear which is so manifest in the other work he has given to the public. His work is distinguished by patient research, and this exact study must do much to make the true principles of S. Ignatius' disciples better known."

In active preparation

S. AMBROSE

By the DUC DE BROGLIE, of the French Academy.

S. JEROME

By the Rev. FR. LARGENT, of the Oratory.

Further volumes will be announced in due course.

Sm. Cr. 8vo, Scarlet Art Vellum, Gilt lettered, gold top.

Irish News.—"The general aim of the series, to bring the lives of the Saints into closer touch with the thought and feeling of the modern Catholic, renders these well-written and well translated little books more instructive and more attractive than some former lives of the Saints."

THE PSYCHOLOGY OF THE SAINTS

By HENRI JOLY, formerly Professor at the Sorbonne and at the Collège de France. Author of "L'homme et l'animal"; "Psychologie des grands hommes," etc.

Pall Mall Gazette.—"A very temperate and admirably reasoned book. There is nothing needlessly or offensively polemical about it, and it may be read with interest by any one. As a kind of general introduction to the whole series the book is all that could be desired."

Month.—"A step in the direction of an intelligent study of phenomena usually accompanying extraordinary sanctity. More than this, it has an indirect, but very real, ascetical value. The English translation is lucid, direct, and altogether readable."

Tablet.—"His book is one which deserves serious attention. We have outrun our space, and must content ourselves in conclusion with warmly recommending M. Joly's work to all who are interested—as what Catholic is not—in the lives of the Saints."

Outlook.—"It is interesting and valuable to the general student. This is an able book; which—even to those far removed from the author's standpoint —will provide food for information, reflection, and discussion."

Catholic Herald.—"If the rest of the volumes are going to reach anything like the level of this, the first of the series, we shall have a small library of hagiology the like of which has never yet been published in England. One of the most remarkable and valuable contributions to the literature of hagiology that has been published in recent years."

Academy.—"A very ably-written little book. A clever and valuable attempt to apply modern methods to ancient problems. M. Joly comes to his difficult task unusually well-equipped. He is helped by science; he is helped, also, by his study of the psychology of genius. This latter is a peculiar advantage for his task, which he shares with no previous student of the subject that we can recollect."

Church Review.—"As a study of what is noblest, purest, and best in humanity, it is bright, cheerful, and invigorating."

Weekly Register (leading article).—"To humanise the Saints in a wider and broader way, founded on a more comprehensive survey of human powers, is the task which has been essayed by M. Joly. This object is brought out by Fr. Tyrrell, S.J., in an admirable preface, possessing the literary touch to a degree not over-common in modern religious writings."

S. AUGUSTINE

By AD. HATZFELD, joint-collaborator with Arsène Darmesteter in the "Dictionnaire Général de la Langue Française." Translated by E. HOLT.

Times.—"We shall rejoice if this little book awakens an interest in a great mind."

The Month.—"The general result will be the familiarising of the ordinary educated public with the true personality of one who is to so many little more than a name. Here, too, the translation of E. Holt is much to be commended for simplicity and good taste. Like all work so far issued by Messrs Duckworth & Co., both volumes are produced with perfect taste in point of binding and printing, and at an exceedingly moderate price."

Literature.—"M. Hatzfeld's excellent life."

Catholic Herald.—"A popular book, a book for the people; but unlike many popular books, it is thoroughly reliable and accurate, the fruit of sound scholarship and wide learning."

Outlook.—"A distinct departure in hagiology. Its plan is unique. The method is very skilfully and judiciously managed, and the result much more interesting than a life constructed on the ordinary plan. The whole book may be unreservedly commended as an excellent and compendious account of Augustine's life and introduction to his works, stripped of controversial matter or needless personal comment."

Manchester Guardian.—"A particularly interesting account of the life and thought of the great Latin father. The man and the saint and the theologian live on his well-written pages."

S. VINCENT DE PAUL

By Prince EMMANUEL DE BROGLIE, Lauréat de l'Académie française. Translated by MILDRED PARTRIDGE.

Literary World.—"A life that should be read by all who can appreciate the saintship of noble work. It would argue a dulness of appreciation quite unbecoming an age that prides itself on historical justice not to recognise in S. Vincent de Paul a Catholic biography that has really Catholic attractiveness, and, what is better, Catholic inspiration."

Dublin Express.—"Those who wish for a plain and sufficiently detailed biography of S. Vincent de Paul will find it here in a neat and cheap outward form."

Scotsman.—"An excellent biography. His story is one of absorbing interest, and it is no light event that the life-story of such a man should be put within reach of the general reader in the form of a piece of good literary workmanship."

Irish News.—"S. Vincent de Paul's character and labours, of lasting interest to every student of heroic benevolence, are sketched in a very graphic manner."

Manchester Guardian.—"Well written and well translated."

S. CLOTILDA

By GODEFROY KURTH, Professor at the University of Liège. Author of "Histoire poétique des Mérovingiens," "Clovis," etc. Translated by V. M. CRAWFORD.

Monitor.—"Professor Kurth has done his utmost to give us a clear idea of life under the Merovingians, and has been able to give to his life of S. Clotilda the touch of grace and interest which assures its success. This is a book which all can read. We can but wish every success to this third volume."

Scotsman.—"Altogether an interesting and instructive life-story."

Catholic Times.—"Mrs Crawford has translated the life with her usual ability, putting it into English which is lucid from beginning to end and undefiled by foreign intermixtures."

Ave Maria.—"A biography that is as authentic as it is fascinating. The translation is all that could be desired."

NEW BOOK BY MADAME BELLOC

HISTORIC NUNS

By B. R. BELLOC, Author of "In a Walled Garden," etc. Crown 8vo, art vellum, gilt, gold top.

In this book Madame Belloc tells the story of four remarkable women who lived and worked in the cause of charity and education during the first half of the present century. Two of them were subjects of our Queen, a third belonged to a noted family in France, and the fourth was daughter to Dr Bayley, Physician to the Royalist forces under Lord Howe in America at the time of the Revolution. All the four achieved permanent results, and the Institutes they founded are still among the most vital products of this wonderful century in England and America.

DUCKWORTH & CO.

3 HENRIETTA STREET, COVENT GARDEN, W.C.

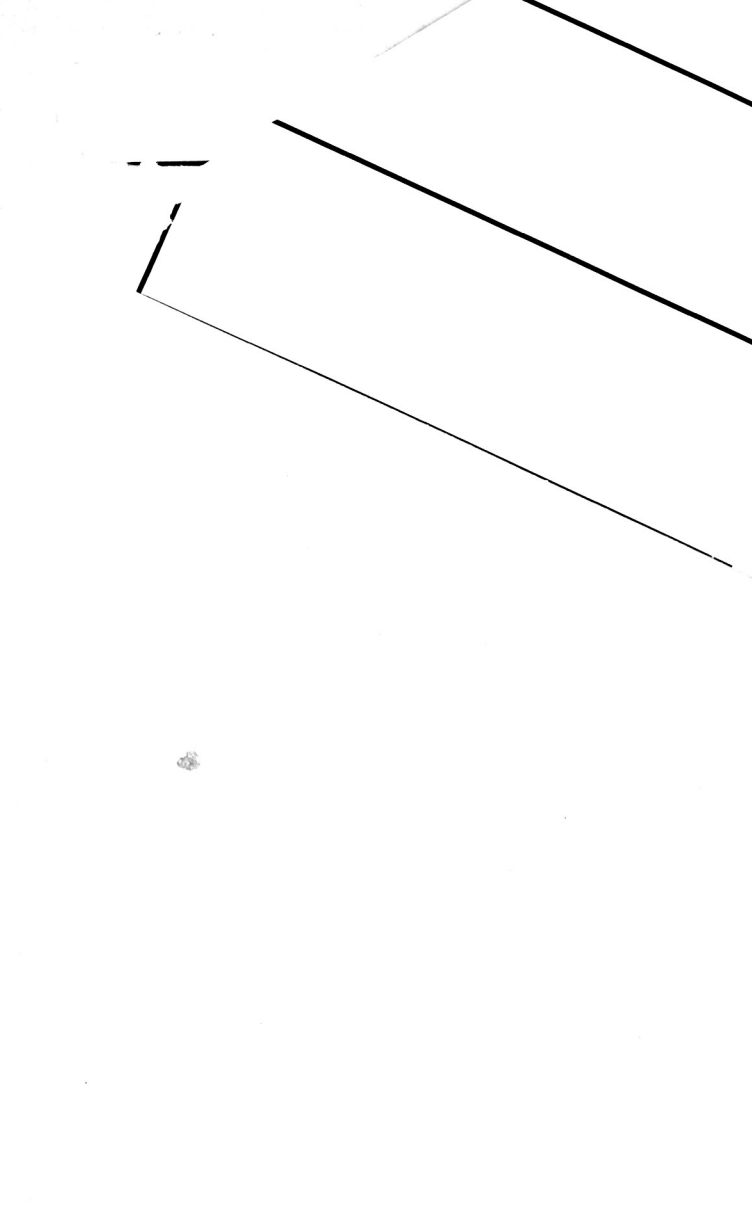